THE 'FORTY-FIVE

The signatures of leading Jacobites. Frontispiece to the Jacobite Correspondence of the Atholl Family, *published by the Abbotsford Club in 1840. (National Library of Scotland)*

THE 'FORTY-FIVE

THE LAST JACOBITE REBELLION

Michael Hook and Walter Ross

THE NATIONAL LIBRARY OF SCOTLAND

HMSO: EDINBURGH

In memory of Kirsty Amro

Designed by Derek Munn, HMSO Graphic Design

Cover photography and styling by Paul Watt and Stephen Kearney, HMSO Photography

Applications for Reproduction should be made to HMSO

British Library Cataloguing in Publication Data
A catalogue record for this book is available from the British Library

ACKNOWLEDGEMENTS

This project began as the result of a chance conversation with our former colleague Ms Jacqueline Cromarty of the National Library of Scotland's Publications Division, and from the start it has been ably steered by her colleague, Dr Ken Gibson. Mr Alastair Cherry of the National Library's Antiquarian Books Division has given us the benefit of his wide knowledge of printed matter relating to the various Jacobite rebellions, and, together with Miss Margaret Wilkes and the staff of the Map Library, offered valuable help in locating relevant illustrations. We have received a great deal of assistance, over a long period, from all the staff of the National Library's Readers' Services Division and the North Reading Room, but owe a special debt to Mrs Barbara Hegarty and Ms Carol Forbes of the Publications Division for their unstinting efforts in gathering illustrations.

Outwith the National Library, Dr Rosalind K Marshall kindly read the first draft of the text, and we are particularly grateful to her for much useful advice and guidance. We are obliged to Mr Francis Maxwell of Kirkconnell for allowing us access to the manuscript left by his ancestor, James Maxwell; and our copy-editor, Ms Stephanie Pickering, deserves an honourable mention for her firm patience in correcting our occasional eccentricities of expression. The staffs of the following institutions have also provided us with valuable assistance: the Edinburgh Room and the Scottish Library at Edinburgh Central Library; the Historical Search Room and the National Register of Archives (Scotland) at the Scottish Record Office; the National Gallery of Scotland. Mrs Suzanna Kerr of the Scottish National Portrait Gallery aided us in sifting through the Blaikie Collection, and helped us to trace portraits of a number of prominent figures. Mr David Mason prepared maps specially for the book. Mr Stephen Kearney and Mr Paul Watt of HMSO were responsible for a number of the location photographs, and Mr Steve McAvoy of the National Library of Scotland and Mr Jack McKenzie of AIC Photographic Services photographed many of the older printed items reproduced in the book.

We would also like to thank the White Cockade Society, and the Talish Gallery, 108 Canongate, Edinburgh, for the period items featured on the cover.

Michael Hook and Walter Ross

Back cover picture: Prince Charles Edward Stuart (1732), by Antonio David. (Scottish National Portrait Gallery)

THE AUTHORS

Michael Hook teaches history at Dornoch Academy, Sutherland. Walter Ross is a researcher and author. In the 1980s they collaborated on the popular historical magazine, the *New Caledonian Mercury* for Scotland's Cultural Heritage in the University of Edinburgh, where they also edited a number of books on Scottish history, including *Lord Provost George Drummond 1687-1766* and *Scots in Russia, 1661-1934*.

ISBN 0 11 495721 5

CONTENTS

The threat of invasion 1744-45, and Prince Charles Edward Stuart's route from Nantes to Eriskay on board the Du Teillay, July 1745.

PREFACE

ON 23 July 1745 Prince Charles Edward Stuart stepped ashore on the island of Eriskay in the Outer Hebrides, to commence what was to be the final attempt to restore the Stuarts to the throne of Great Britain. Having been born in Rome, the prince was setting foot on British soil for the first time at the age of twenty-four. Almost sixty years had passed since his grandfather, James II, had fled the country, after being deposed in favour of a Protestant monarch, but the Young Pretender (as he was widely known) hoped to take advantage of the European war that was raging to start a rising, and overthrow the Whig constitution from within. His small flotilla of privateers had just been intercepted at sea by the Royal Navy, and Charles arrived in Scotland without the foreign troops or arms he had promised to bring. Instead, he sought support among leading Highland chieftains by appealing directly to their loyalty. Having gained it, he almost succeeded in pushing George II, the Elector of Hanover, off the throne of the United Kingdom.

In a matter of weeks, the scant government forces in Scotland were first outmanoeuvred and then overrun at the battle of Prestonpans, leaving the capital, Edinburgh, at the rebels' mercy. While one Jacobite army held large tracts of the central Highlands, the prince led another army into England to rally Jacobites there, and link up with a French invasion. He reached Derby in the English Midlands before his hopes of assistance were dashed and he was forced to retrace his steps. Thereafter the rising in Scotland took on the aspect of a civil war. It witnessed the last pitched battles fought in Britain, culminating in the disastrous defeat inflicted on the rebels by the Duke of Cumberland at Culloden in April 1746, after which the government embarked on a campaign of barbarous executions and other savage reprisals. Prince Charles became the quarry in perhaps the most famous manhunt in history — wandering the western Highlands and Islands throughout the following summer — before escaping into exile from Arisaig late in September.

These are the bare bones of a story which for two-and-a-half centuries has continued to fascinate. If it is at all regrettable that this fascination has found an outlet in the tartan-and-lace finery associated with ceilidhs and shortbread tins, the curiosity provoked by the clash of irreconcilable passions and opinions underlying the '45 has nevertheless turned *Bliadhna Thierlaich* (Charlie's Year) into one of the best documented struggles for power in European history. Setting aside romantic views of it, *The 'Forty-Five — The Last Jacobite Rebellion* uses both contemporary sources and secondary works drawn from the National Library of Scotland's vast collection of manuscripts and printed books, to piece together the history of the rising; and, because they are aspects which are often neglected, it pays particular attention to the international background against which the insurrection took place, and the way events were reported in the press. In an effort to give a flavour of the period, a number of documents from the Library's Walter Biggar Blaikie Collection* and other special collections are reproduced in colour, along with many portraits, engravings and artefacts connected with the rebellion.

Michael Hook and Walter Ross

(*While owned by the National Library of Scotland, a significant part of the Blaikie Collection of Jacobite material is on long-term deposit with the Scottish National Portrait Gallery. Items falling into this category are credited 'National Library of Scotland; on loan to the Scottish National Portrait Gallery'.)

NOTE ON DATES AND SPELLING

GIVING accurate dates for international affairs before 1752 is complicated by the fact that until that year Great Britain and its Dominions used the Julian or Old Style calendar, which was eleven days behind the Gregorian or New Style calendar in widespread use in contintental Europe. The custom is followed here of using Old Style to date events during the fourteen months or so that Prince Charles spent in the British Isles. All other dates are New Style.

It is worth emphasising — because it is easily overlooked — that English was not the first language of many of those who fought on the opposing sides in the rebellion of 1745-46. Although large numbers of foreign mercenaries were employed by the British government, the mishmash of languages and accents spoken by the Jacobites — Gaelic, English, French and Spanish — must have handicapped their efforts in particular, because almost every stage in the campaign involved the leadership in wrangles over policy. Even where they spoke the same language, it is not difficult to imagine how strain might have arisen between men who expressed themselves so differently in it as, for instance, Lord George Murray and John William O'Sullivan did. To preserve these contrasts (with the exception of a few instances where the sense would otherwise be unclear) the original spelling and punctuation have been retained in quoted passages.

PRINCE CHARLES EDWARD STUART
AND THE BRITISH ROYAL FAMILY

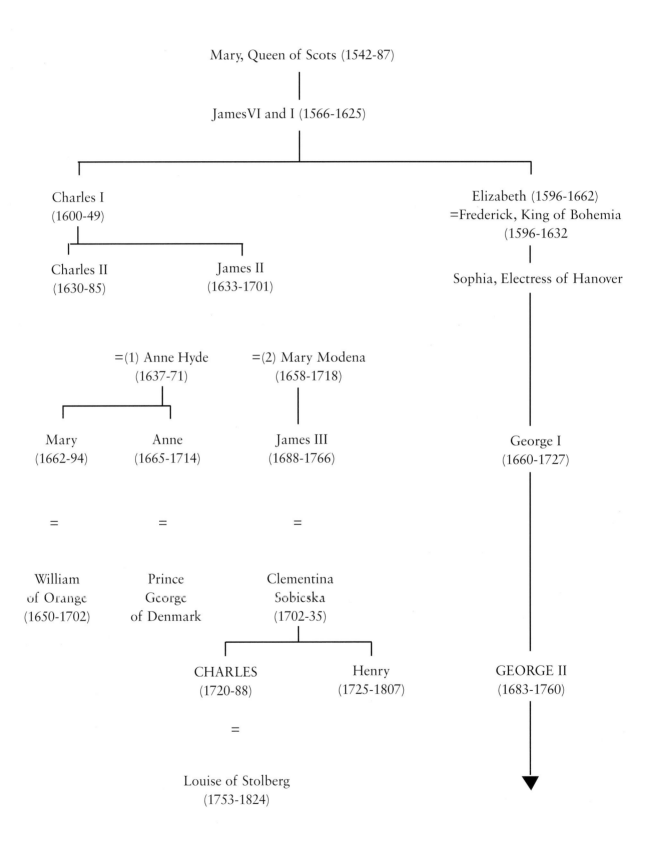

1 ORIGINS

In our present situation we have no other solid hope for our Restoration but from the French and the Resolutions of Court: that depend chiefly, if not solely, in what relates to England and not Scotland. You know that we can do nothing for ourselves without a certain number of foreign troops, and whenever France may think fit to give them, our case becomes theirs and they will not stand it.
(JAMES III TO CHARLES EDWARD, 30 MARCH 1745)

IN December 1688 James II of Great Britain fled to France and sought sanctuary at the court of his cousin, Louis XIV. James's ignominious departure, only three years after ascending to the throne, was the result of his own political ineptitude. During his brief reign, James had managed to alienate practically all sections of society in both Scotland and England, largely as a result of his dogged determination to restore Roman Catholicism to both these countries. In open defiance of the law, James appointed fellow Roman Catholics to senior positions in the army, navy, government and the universities. Moreover, in order to ensure that his policies were implemented, James refused to consult parliament (which he had prorogued at the start of his reign), and ruled by what amounted to royal decree. To many people, James's actions smacked of the absolutism of Louis XIV's France, and opposition to the king and his policies became widespread.

James's fate was finally decided when, on 10 June 1688, his wife gave birth to a son, James Francis Edward. Until then, the king's opponents had consoled themselves with the knowledge that, on James's death, the crowns of England, Scotland and Ireland would pass to his Protestant daughter, Mary, who was married to William of Orange. With the birth of James Francis, now heir-apparent, this Protestant succession could no longer be guaranteed; few doubted that the young prince would be raised as a Roman Catholic, thereby ensuring that James's reforms would become permanent. To prevent this from happening, a group of influential English statesmen appealed to William of Orange for assistance. William, ever anxious to obtain new allies in his struggle with Louis XIV, readily agreed, and on 5 November the Dutch prince landed at Torbay in Devonshire at the head of 14,000 Protestant mercenaries.

When Englishmen throughout the country rallied to William's standard, James was unable to assemble an adequate force to oppose him. Rather than risk defeat in battle, he fled to France, thereby condemning the Stuart

Prince James Francis Edward Stuart (1688-1766), the Old Pretender. The only surviving son of James VII and Mary of Modena, he was recognised by Jacobites as James III of England and VIII of Scotland following his father's death in 1701. Painted by François de Troy in 1701. (Scottish National Portrait Gallery)

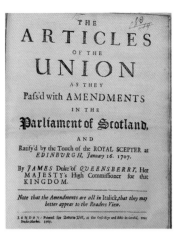

The Articles of Union between the Parliaments of Scotland and England were drawn up by Commissioners in 1706, and the Treaty and Act of Union came into force on 1 May 1707. (National Library of Scotland, Hall 195.f.6 (1-30))

dynasty to permanent exile. The so-called 'Glorious Revolution' was finally consolidated when the English, and later the Scots, offered their respective crowns to William and Mary. In 1701 the English parliament passed the Act of Settlement which vested the succession to the English throne in the Protestant House of Hanover, something the Scots were later forced to accept under the terms of the 1707 Treaty of Union.

But despite the events of 1688–9 and the subsequent parliamentary legislation, the Stuarts never gave up hope of regaining the three kingdoms. When James II died in 1701 his son was recognised as James III of Great Britain by his supporters, although his enemies disparagingly referred to him as the 'Old Pretender' (after the French word *prétendant* meaning 'claimant'). On 31 December 1720, James's wife, Clementina Sobieska, gave birth to a son who was christened Charles Edward Louis John Casimir Silvester Xavier Maria. Although he was born and raised in Rome, Charles Edward's driving ambition was to oust the Hanoverian dynasty and win back his father's throne; but, in the years following the prince's birth, the possibility of a Stuart restoration appeared increasingly unlikely.

In October 1736 James wrote to the Duke of Ormonde confessing, 'I see no appearance of our being able to do anything for ourselves there without foreign force.' This was simply a reiteration of well-established Jacobite policy: by the 1720s it had become clear to the exiled monarch that foreign assistance would be required if he was ever to regain his crown. There had been a number of serious setbacks to the cause, beginning with the failure of

The Westminster Parliament's ratification of the Treaty of Union, as sent to Scotland. In manifestos written prior to the '45 the Stuarts concurred with the view of many Scots that the Union was unacceptable in its present form, but they astutely left it to a future 'free Parliament' to decide what should replace it. (By permission of the Keeper of the Records of Scotland)

the rising that had taken place in 1715, and continuing with the débâcle of 1719, the discovery of the Atterbury Plot (1722) and, finally, the peaceful accession of George II in 1727. The failure of home-based Jacobites to exploit these opportunities meant that James had little option but to turn to sympathetic European powers for support.

Unfortunately for the Stuart king, the 1720s and 1730s were not the most propitious decades for him to seek and obtain military backing. Frustratingly for the Jacobites, Britain remained at peace throughout this period, having signed a formal alliance with France in 1716 which survived, somewhat precariously, until 1731. Even after 1731, Britain, under the guidance of Sir Robert Walpole, and France, directed by Cardinal Fleury, were reluctant to jeopardise their respective domestic and foreign policies by engaging in mutual hostilities — Britain even remaining aloof during the Polish Succession War (1733–5) in which France participated. France was always regarded by the Jacobites as being the nation most likely to provide assistance, given her traditional distrust and fear of Britain's growing naval, commercial and financial power. The British government was acutely aware that France would face fewer logistical difficulties in mounting an invasion than any other European country, and any movement of troops in or around the French Channel ports provoked a near hysterical reaction on the other side of the water.

By deeming a traitor's blood attainted, English law prevented his property, estates or titles passing to his descendants after his death. Despite widespread opposition, this law was extended to Scotland after the Union of the Parliaments. (National Library of Scotland, MS.2960, f.50)

Landinge en inhalinge van de Pretendent tot PETER HEAD in Schotland; onder de naam van Koning IACO BUS de VIII van Schotland, en de III van Engeland, op den 2 Ianuary 1716.

IACOBI ejus nominis cicti octavi Regnum Bri tanniarium adfectantis, adventus in Scotiam postrie. kal. Ianuar 1716.

Pet Schenk exc. Amst. Cum privi.

An engraving showing the arrival of the Old Pretender at Peterhead in December 1715. By then the battle of Sheriffmuir had already been fought and the rising was effectively over. (National Library of Scotland; on loan to the Scottish National Portrait Gallery)

After the 1715 rising was crushed, many of the Scottish prisoners were marched over the border to face trial in England, a step which met with disquiet in Scotland. (National Library of Scotland; on loan to the Scottish National Portrait Gallery)

The alliance between France and Britain served to thwart the Jacobites, but did not prevent them seeking succour elsewhere. Sweden, Russia, Austria and Spain were all approached during this period whenever it appeared to the Jacobite envoys that there was a serious deterioration in their diplomatic relations with Britain. Spain did provide military assistance during the 1719 rising, but a combination of bad weather, superior British naval power and divided Jacobite leadership turned the whole affair into a fiasco, ending in defeat for the Jacobites at Glenshiel. What James and his advisers consistently failed to appreciate during negotiations with foreign powers was that the leaders of these nations, no matter how sympathetic they might have been to James's cause, would only agree to provide help if and when it was in their interest to do so: no country wished to risk war with Britain with the sole objective of restoring the Stuarts. On the vast European stage, where the main players were kings, queens and emperors who ruled over large and powerful states, James Stuart could only ever have a walk-on part; nevertheless, he was still a member of the cast and, as such, capable of stealing a scene. But for that to happen, Britain needed to be involved in a major conflict with another continental power — preferably France.

Jacobite hopes were raised with the outbreak of the War of the Austrian Succession in 1740. To begin with, however, neither Britain nor France was officially at war with the other: British policy centred on providing financial support for Austria while the French sponsored Bavaria and Spain. Yet still Fleury and Walpole drew back from outright confrontation, even though French troops crossed the Rhine during the summer of 1741. Fleury was inundated with proposals from both Scottish and English Jacobites advocating an immediate French invasion of Britain, proposals which wildly exaggerated the strength of Jacobite support the French could expect on landing. While not actively discouraging these reports, Fleury chose to ignore them.

The situation changed dramatically with the resignation of Sir Robert Walpole in February 1742, following the government's poor showing in the 1741 general election. In the subsequent reshuffle of the ministry, John

The Baptism of Prince Charles Edward Stuart at the Muti Palace in Rome, by Pier Leone Ghezzi and Agostino Masucci. (Scottish National Portrait Gallery)

Carteret, later Earl Granville, was appointed Secretary of State for the Northern Department and effectively controlled British foreign policy in Europe until his resignation in 1744. Carteret pursued a vigorously anti-French line, as evinced by his decision to send British troops into the Austrian Netherlands later that year. Cardinal Fleury's death in January 1743, coupled with France's forced withdrawal from Bavaria and the defeat of another French army under the Duc de Noailles at Dettingen in June, paved the way for French intervention on behalf of James. France was now in serious danger of invasion, Carteret employing all his diplomatic skills to persuade Charles Albert of Bavaria to abandon France and seek territorial gains at the expense of his former ally. These serious military reversals persuaded Louis XV of the need to strike a decisive blow against George II (who had commanded the allies at Dettingen), thus relieving the pressure on his forces in Europe.

An early portrait of Prince Charles in martial attire. (National Library of Scotland; on loan to the Scottish National Portrait Gallery)

By late 1743, Louis had finalised his plans: France would mount a cross-Channel invasion of England with the aim of restoring the Stuarts, thereby ensuring that Britain would take no further part in the war. France's most able general, Hermann Maurice, Comte de Saxe and 10,000 troops were to embark at Dunkirk in a fleet of transports, cross the Channel and land at Maldon in Essex where they would be joined by English Jacobites. From Maldon the combined forces would march on London and seize the capital before the English authorities could react. Charles Edward Stuart left Rome on 9 January 1744 and arrived at Paris on 8 February. The prince's presence was considered essential, if only to provide an air of legitimacy to the expedition: France, after all, was still not officially at war with Britain.

After a number of unforeseen delays, Admiral de Roquefeuil finally set sail from Brest with twenty-two ships of the line. His mission was to engage Admiral Norris in the western Channel so as to prevent the British fleet from intercepting the invasion force. But Norris, whom de Roquefeuil expected to find at Spithead, had already left with instructions to stop the French transports from leaving Dunkirk. De Roquefeuil followed his enemy up the Channel where, in the teeth of a howling gale, the two fleets confronted one another off Dungeness on 7 March. The storms prevented the two fleets from engaging, the wind scattering Norris's ships while the French were able to run before the gale and return to Brest. At Dunkirk the same storms caused considerable damage to the waiting fleet of transports, a number of which were sunk with all hands. Saxe was incensed. He complained furiously that his men should have already landed in England, but that he had been forced to delay his departure because the English pilots, who were to have guided him ashore at Blackwall in the Thames estuary (the rearranged landfall), had not arrived, nor, indeed, had his naval escort of five ships from the Brest fleet. Protesting that to continue was now pointless, Saxe demanded that the whole expedition be called off. While the commander's political masters hesitated, nature again intervened: on 11 March a second storm hit the transports, resulting in further serious damage. On the very same day, Saxe wrote to Charles Edward, then at Gravelines, informing him that the undertaking was cancelled. Nine days later, France formally declared war on Britain.

Cardinal André Hercule de Fleury (1653-1743), who guided French foreign affairs from 1726 until his death. Fleury's antagonism towards the Jacobites helped ensure peace between Britain and France throughout the 1720s and 1730s. (National Library of Scotland; on loan to the Scottish National Portrait Gallery)

With the failure of the invasion attempt, Charles Edward Stuart now took centre stage, for the Jacobite rising of 1745 stemmed directly from the events of March 1744. Charles's immediate reaction was predictable: frustrated and bitterly disappointed, he sought an interview with Saxe to try and persuade him to reverse his decision. When this was not forthcoming, the prince then blamed the expedition's failure on French incompetence and cowardice. This was grossly unfair: the military and naval preparations for the invasion had been extensive and, while the risks involved in mounting a cross-Channel invasion were always going to be considerable, there could be no denying French commitment — as Louis XV's personal involvement with the project clearly demonstrated. As Saxe suggested to Charles, if a scapegoat had to be found then the prince would be as well blaming Dame Fortune since he, Saxe, had no control over the elements.

Charles, despite his obvious disappointment, still recognised how important French military support was if any future attempt to restore James was to succeed — the English Jacobites in particular had made this a necessary pre-condition of their rising in favour of his father. The French, on the other hand, required more than verbal assurances to persuade them that another invasion attempt was feasible: actions rather than words were

Sir Robert Walpole (1676-1745) was Whig prime minister for the first twenty-one years of Prince Charles's life. Supporters of the government prospered, while Tories, Jacobites and religious non-conformists were subjected to discrimination, and excluded from posts and offices in the gift of the crown, including army commissions. (Copyright British Museum)

The General Election of 1741: Whig bribes lure a drowsy electorate to the edge of a precipice. Nowhere did the financial corruption and jobbery under Walpole provoke more outrage than in the Highlands, where the thin trickle of government patronage in Scotland petered out. (Copyright British Museum)

necessary, but neither side was prepared to act before the other. Resolving this dilemma was the major difficulty facing Charles Edward in the aftermath of the expedition's failure when, with his customary refusal to contemplate potential pitfalls, he arrived at what seemed an obvious and simple solution.

Aware that Scotland, and in particular the Highlands of Scotland, had traditionally been the most fertile recruiting ground for the Stuarts, Charles considered the possibility of an unsupported landing in Scotland which, if successful, would both force the French to intervene on his behalf and also galvanise the English Jacobites into action. The first indication of the prince's intentions came shortly after the invasion had been called off. Still smarting from a sense of betrayal, Charles tried to persuade George Keith, Earl Marischal and one of James's most trusted advisers, to accompany him to Scotland where, together, they would raise the loyal clans. Not surprisingly, Marischal refused to have anything to do with such an absurd idea, and did his best to dissuade the prince from entertaining further notions of an unsupported landing in Scotland, or anywhere else. Marischal's advice was merely an echo of the sentiments of his royal master in Rome. Although unhappy about the way in which his son had been treated by the French, James urged Charles not to jeopardise the cause through some irresponsible, impetuous action which would only end in disaster. James refused to contemplate an attempt against Scotland alone; for him it was all or nothing. In January 1745 he wrote from Rome: 'It is very true that I have been all along against an expedition upon Scotland alone, or rather, in general, against any faint attempt, the consequences of which might be more fatal to the cause than not attempting any thing at all.'

If the prince's plan was to succeed, then utmost secrecy had to be maintained. Not only would his father actively seek to discourage him, but the French court might very well expel him from the country if his plans were made public. Louis XV was anxious to avoid alienating his German allies, especially Frederick the Great of Prussia, who viewed France's support of the Catholic Stuarts with considerable suspicion. Frederick had no desire to transform the present conflict, which he regarded as a justifiable territorial and dynastic struggle, into a war of religion. Consequently, Charles was forced to remain incognito while he resided in France and, in order to prevent him from obtaining an audience with Louis (which would have been diplomatically embarrassing to the king under the circumstances) the Stuart prince was effectively banned from Paris and Versailles. This ban was flouted by the prince on a number of occasions: he took an almost childlike delight in attending social events in the capital in open defiance of ministerial wishes, which further alienated his French hosts. But this defiance was a result of the prince's own frustration. As the summer of 1744 wore on it became increasingly obvious, even to Charles, that there was no serious possibility of further French aid that year. Rather than return, humiliated, to Rome having achieved nothing, Charles determined to

George Keith, 10th Earl Marischal (1693-1778), by Cosmo Alexander. He participated in the 1715 rising but his personal antipathy to Prince Charles kept him out of the '45. (Scottish National Portrait Gallery)

press ahead with his plans. Colonel John William O'Sullivan, one of the 'Seven Men of Moidart', later summed up Charles's position:

> The Prince being dissatisfied with the treatment he had from the Court of France, & finding yt the Frinch Ministry had no real design to restablish the King, was resol'd at any reat, to try what his presence cou'd do among his friends at home, without any other succor, & imagening at the same time, if he cou'd come to make a head, & have the least good success or advantage, yt yt wou'd engage the Frinch Court to send him a real succor. John Murray's arrival at Paris confirmed, as it is said, H.R.H.s in this resolution, & assur'd him, as I am told, yt the King's friends wou'd receive him with open Arms; & yt he did not even doubt but they wou'd surprise all the fortes and Castles of Scotland, wch wou'd procure him armes & ammunition, & by those means wou'd be Mastre of Scotland without being oblidged to draw a Sword.

If the need for secrecy was important, then the backing of the Scottish Jacobites was crucial, which is why the meeting between Murray and the prince referred to by O'Sullivan deserves special attention. The discussions took place in August 1744 while Charles was staying at the house of Aeneas Macdonald in Paris. John Murray of Broughton was the son of Sir David Murray of Stanhope, a Jacobite laird of 'great honour and worth', and, since 1740, had acted as official correspondent between James and the 'Association' — a group of leading Scottish Jacobites.

According to Murray, the purpose of his meeting with Charles was to 'lay a state before him of what had passed…the false and contradictory intelligence sent us…and finally to learn what had put a stop to the [French] embarkation, what situation affairs were then in, and what steps his friends in Scotland were to take'. That the Scots had been kept in such ignorance of affairs in France was seen by many as being the fault of two of James's most active envoys in Paris — William Drummond (alias Macgregor) of Balhaldie, and Francis, Lord Sempill. Murray was particularly severe in his condemnation of their actions, accusing both of deliberately misleading Charles and of attempting to isolate him from his loyal followers, 'knowing that if he [Charles] had access to hear such, their underhand dealings would be discovered, and they either dismissed or disregarded'.

In a private audience with the prince, Murray was encouraged to speak openly. He accused Sempill and Balhaldie of falsifying intelligence to suit their own purposes and of exaggerating the level of support that Charles might expect from Scotland — 20,000 men according to Balhaldie. The prince, however, refused to condemn either man outright, but merely expressed concern that his Scottish supporters felt themselves 'imposed upon'. Charles also spoke of his conviction that Louis would provide him with troops to mount another expedition before the onset of winter. When Murray cogently argued that French military assistance was extremely unlikely given the situation in Flanders, where the French army had been forced onto the defensive, the prince replied that he was 'determined to come

Louis XV (1710-1774), by Maurice Quentin de La Tour. (Musée du Louvre, Département des Arts Graphiques)

the following summer to Scotland, though with a single footman'. Murray was appalled by this statement. He urged Charles not to come to Scotland alone as without French troops the prince 'could not positively depend on more than 4000 Highlanders' to support him. In reply, Charles offered to 'try every method to procure troops; but should that fail, he would, nevertheless pay us a visit'. If we are to accept Murray's version of the meeting rather than O'Sullivan's (which must have been based on hearsay), then it is clear that Charles was determined to press ahead with his plans despite all Murray's best efforts on the Association's behalf to dissuade him from such a course of action.

Despite his misgivings, Murray agreed to inform the Association of the prince's intentions and returned to Scotland in October. Somewhat

THE
Fatal Consequences

To be feared (if not speedily prevented) by our assisting the Queen of Hungary, and the King of Sardinia in the Mediterraneau, and on the Coasts of Italy, and from the Treaty we entered into with Them at Worms in September 1743.

AND LIKEWISE
The Danger of keeping our Lord Mercenary Hanoverian Troops in the Pay, when they are not in the Service, of Great Britain.

AS ALSO
The imminent Danger of employing our Naval Force in the Service of Foreigners, and exposing our own Trade to the Depredation of Spain, and leaving our own Coast naked and open to the Insults (if not to the Invasion) of France.

Printed in the YEAR M.DCC.XLIV.
And sold at the Pamphlet-Shops in London and Westminster.

13

During the War of the Austrian Succession, troops and gold were sent overseas in support of George II's possessions in Hanover. The resentment this aroused in Britain was misconstrued by Jacobite agents as evidence of widespread opposition to government policy on the war. (National Library of Scotland, Ry.1.2.85(13))

George II (1683-1760), painted in 1744 by Thomas Hudson. The king spoke German fluently and spent part of every summer in his Electorate of Hanover. He was abroad when Prince Charles landed on Eriskay in July 1745. (By courtesy of the National Portrait Gallery, London)

predictably, the leading Scottish Jacobites' reaction to Murray's news was one of dismay. With the exception of the Duke of Perth, whose loyalty to the Stuarts was unshakeable, all sought to dissuade the prince from coming to Scotland the following year unless he was accompanied by French troops. A letter to this effect was sent to Charles in the care of Lord Traquair who, inexplicably, failed to deliver it, the unopened letter being returned to Murray in April 1745.

Meanwhile, Charles pressed ahead with his plans. There were two major obstacles in his path — lack of money and of transport. With French assistance unlikely to be forthcoming, Charles would somehow have to raise money himself to purchase arms and ammunition for the Highland clans (always assuming they would rise), who were in desperate need of both. He managed to borrow 40,000 *livres* from George Waters, the Paris banker, to pay for broadswords which, as he explained to his father, might be needed at short notice if the French should suddenly change their minds and order another invasion of Britain. James reluctantly agreed and sent a letter of credit to cover the sum borrowed. Waters, delighted with the speed at which James had responded, extended Charles's credit to 120,000 *livres* enabling the prince to buy more arms. By June 1745 he had amassed a substantial arsenal and the sum of 4000 *louis d'or*, which were stored in a warehouse at Nantes.

Having managed to procure arms for the expedition, Charles was now faced with the greater challenge of securing transport. Obtaining a ship, as O'Sullivan pointed out, 'was no easy matter, without the help or knowledge of the Frinch Court, whom he had his raisons not to let into the secret of his project, nor even the King our Mastre, fearing least his Majesty, wou'd oppose it'. However, help was to come from an unlikely source — a group of Franco-Irish shipowners based at Nantes and St Malo. This swashbuckling clique of adventurers had grown wealthy through smuggling, privateering and the slave-trade, and were in the business of making money, whatever the risk. More importantly for Charles, they had a lifetime's experience of hoodwinking the French naval authorities, who tolerated their activities because of the privateers' ability to disrupt British shipping in times of war. These men were introduced to the prince by the Jacobite peer Charles O'Brien, Viscount Clare. Of particular importance were Sir Walter Ruttledge and Antoine Walsh, both of whom were familiar with the practice of using French men-of-war for privateering expeditions.

In April 1745, realising that Walsh and Ruttledge's activities would provide the ideal cover for his own enterprise, the prince discussed the possibility of using the *Elisabeth*, a 64-gun French man-of-war commissioned by Ruttledge for a privateering expedition in the North Sea, to convey him to Scotland. Ruttledge passed on Charles's ideas to Walsh, who immediately agreed to the project and put his own ship, the frigate *Du Teillay*, at the prince's disposal. Both Walsh and Ruttledge were taking a considerable financial risk in backing the prince, but it was a risk each was prepared to accept as the rewards which would accrue to them on the successful restoration of the Stuarts would be enormous. Financial gain was not the sole motivation behind Walsh's decision however: the Irishman was to remain a loyal supporter of the cause until his death in 1759, and his devotion to Charles was absolute.

By the end of April, then, the prince's dream was well on the way to becoming a reality. With transport secured and an adequate arsenal assembled, the prince now had to select his companions for the voyage. The choice was relatively easy, if only because Charles had confided in very few of his associates. The most senior in terms of rank (if not age) was William Murray, Marquis of Tullibardine. Eldest surviving son of John, 1st Duke of Atholl, Tullibardine had been attainted for his part in both the '15 and the '19 risings. His younger brother, James, was recognised as Duke of Atholl by the Hanoverians, although the Jacobites still considered William to be the rightful heir, invariably referring to him as 'Duke William'. Fifty-six years of age in 1745, Tullibardine suffered from gout and was described by one contemporary as a 'tottering old man'.

The only other Scot to accompany Charles was the Paris banker Aeneas Macdonald, brother to Macdonald of Kinlochmoidart. Selected for his family and financial connections, it would be difficult to describe Macdonald as an ardent Jacobite, but he was persuaded to travel with the prince as he had been going to Scotland on business in any event. Francis Strickland was the sole Englishman in the prince's party. A former tutor to Charles's brother Prince Henry, Strickland came from an old Westmorland family with strong Jacobite ties. The two Scots and the Englishman were accompanied by four Irishmen, Sir Thomas Sheridan, George Kelly, Sir John Macdonald and John William O'Sullivan. Sheridan, a loyal and devoted servant, proved more of a liability than an asset due to his great age, while the Reverend George Kelly — 'a parson and intriguer' — was mistrusted by most and detested by the prince's father. Sir John Macdonald was a captain of carabiniers in the French service whose exploits with the bottle afforded him more of a reputation than his previous military career, which remained somewhat obscure. The remaining Irishman was O'Sullivan, who, despite coming late into the prince's service, was one of his most steadfast and loyal adherents. This almost reverential devotion to Charles, combined with an ill-founded belief in his own military ability, later involved O'Sullivan in many rancorous disputes with Lord George Murray and divided the Jacobite high command. Ultimately these divisions were to prove fatal.

These, then, were the legendary 'Seven Men of Moidart'. A more unlikely band of revolutionaries is hard to imagine: most were well past their physical prime and only three had any military experience to speak of. Five of the seven had no knowledge whatsoever of the Highlands or its inhabitants. Overall, their contribution to the rising was either negligible or, in the case of O'Sullivan, positively damaging. They were not Charles's only companions however. Also on board the *Du Teillay* were Duncan Buchanan, clerk to Aeneas Macdonald; the Abbé Butler, a relative of the Duke of Ormonde, who acted as chaplain to the prince's party during the voyage;

Duncan Cameron, a retainer of the elder Lochiel who was taken along as the ship's pilot, and one Michele Vezzosi, an Italian who claimed to have helped Charles's mother to escape from Innsbruck in April 1719. By 1745 Vezzosi's duties were rather more prosaic: he was entrusted with keeping the prince's accounts during the campaign. Just what Antoine Walsh made of Charles's choice of companions is not recorded, but the Irishman's presence on board was worth more to Charles than all the rest put together.

*****

Before describing Charles Edward's journey to Scotland, it seems appropriate at this stage to examine what it was that James was offering the people of Britain in the event of a restoration. Or, to put it another way, who would benefit from the overthrow of George II. As with modern-day leaders of opposition parties awaiting an opportunity to oust the sitting government, James published a manifesto outlining his vision of Britain under Stuart rule. In fact he had drawn up two separate manifestos, both dated 23 December 1744, when French preparations for the invasion of England were at their height. One manifesto was for Scotland, the other for England and, while differing in style and content, both shared a degree of vagueness over specific policies which would have aroused the admiration and envy of many a twentieth-century politician. Given that the rising centred on Scotland, James's Scottish manifesto deserves closer attention. Having expressed his 'constant affection' for Scotland, James identified the main reason for the country's 'intolerable burdens':

> We see a nation always famous for valour, and highly esteemed by the greatest of foreign potentates, reduced to the condition of a province, under the specious pretence of a union with a more powerful neighbour. In consequence of this pretended union, grievous and unprecedented taxes have been laid on, and levied with severity in spite of all the representations that could be made to the contrary; and these have not failed to produce that poverty and decay of trade which were easily forseen to be the necessary consequences of such oppressive measures.

The solution, according to James, was simple:

> We will with all convenient speed call a free parliament; that by the advice and assistance of such an assembly, we may be enabled to repair the breaches caused by so long an usurpation, to redress all grievances, and to free our people from the unsupportable burden of the malt-tax, and all other hardships and impositions which have been the consequences of the pretended union; that so the nation may be restored to that honour, liberty, and independency, which it formerly enjoyed.

In singling out the Union of 1707 as the root of all Scotland's troubles, the Jacobites clearly hoped to exploit nationalist sentiment and turn it to their advantage. However, it is far from clear just how widespread Scottish 'nationalism' was in 1745. Such an appeal had fallen on fertile ground in 1715 when discontent with the Union was at its zenith, but, as Lord

JAMES R.

WHEREAS we have a near Prospect of being restored to the
Throne of our Ancestors, by the good Inclinations of our
Subjects towards Us; and whereas, on Account of the present Situation of this Country, it will be absolutely impossible for Us to be in Person at the first setting up of our Royal Standard, and even sometime
after. We therefore esteem it for our Service, and the good of Our
Kingdoms and Dominions, to nominate and appoint, as We hereby
nominate, constitute, and appoint Our dearest Son CHARLES, Prince of
Wales, to be sole Regent of our Kingdoms of *England*, *Scotland*, and
Ireland, and of all other our Dominions during our Absence. It is
our Will and Intention, That our said dearest Son should enjoy and
exercise all that Power and Authority, which, according to the ancient Constitution of our Kingdoms, has been enjoyed and exercised by
former Regents. Requiring all our faithful Subjects, to give all due
Submission and Obedience to our Regent aforesaid, as immediately re-
presenting our Royal Person, and acting by our Authority. And We
do hereby revoke all Commissions of Regency, granted to any Person
or Persons whatsoever. And, *lastly*, We hereby dispence with all
Formalities, and other Omissions, that may be herein contained; Declaring this our Commission to be as firm and valid to all Intents and
Purposes, as if it had passed our great Seals, and as if it were according to the usual Stile and Forms. Given under our Sign-manual and
privy Signet, at Our Court at *Rome*, the 23d Day of *December* 1743,
in the Forty third Year of Our Reign.

J. R.

(L. S.)

CHARLES P. R.

BY Virtue and Authority of the above Commission of Regency,
granted unto Us by the King Our Royal Father. We are
now come to execute His Majesty's Will and Pleasure, by setting up
His Royal Standard, and asserting his undoubted Right to the Throne
of his Ancestors.

E

A copy of James's Commission of Regency, dated at Rome on 23 December 1743, conferring on Prince Charles the power to act in his name. (National Library of Scotland, MS 940, f.3)

George Murray remarked, 'Thirty years has made a great alteration in things, in men, and their minds'. And while the Union had not yet brought economic prosperity to Scotland as a whole, the years of relative social stability which had prevailed since 1707 helped to create the necessary confidence for the economic and industrial development which was to follow during the latter half of the century. Moreover, despite James's anti-Union rhetoric, his Scottish manifesto gave no firm guarantee that the Union would be severed in the event of his restoration. This is hardly surprising: James sought restoration to the thrones of Scotland, England and Ireland, and would have preferred — for political, social and economic reasons — to retain the structure of post-1707 Great Britain. But it was England, with her superior resources, manpower and wealth which James coveted above all — the aspirations of the Scots and Irish would always be subordinated to those of the more powerful kingdom. Charles Edward, while sharing his father's ambition to restore the Stuarts to all three kingdoms, was far less circumspect. In a proclamation dated

Prince Charles as a youth, in Polish military uniform. His great-grandfather, King John III of Poland, was famed throughout Europe for his exploits against the Turks at Vienna in 1683. (National Library of Scotland; on loan to the Scottish National Portrait Gallery)

9 October 1745, Charles would respond to George II's summoning of parliament by prohibiting any of his father's Scottish subjects from attending this unlawful 'assembly'. Should individuals refuse to obey the prince's command they would be 'proceeded against as Traitors and Rebels to their King and Country...the pretended Union of these Kingdoms being now at an End'. It is highly unlikely that James would have sanctioned Charles's unilateral decision, and the incident helps to illustrate Stuart ambivalence over the constitutional future of the United Kingdom.

James's English manifesto did not mention the possible abolition of the Union, but a number of the other provisions were similar to those contained in the Scottish version. He promised to maintain and support the established churches in both kingdoms in all their 'rights, privileges, possessions, and immunities whatsoever'. Financial inducements were promised to all those men serving in the armed forces of the 'usurper', including a 'gratification of a whole year's pay' to all sailors and soldiers who would 'employ their arms' in James's service. Under the Stuarts, trade and commerce would flourish, bribery and corruption would be ended, and future foreign policy would be determined by the needs of Britain, not Hanover. James also promised to 'act always by the advice of our parliaments', and to 'value none of our titles so much as that of *common father of our people*'. It seems, then, that James had learned from the past, and was anxious to persuade the peoples of Britain that he would not act in an arbitrary and despotic manner.

The manifestos set out to present James as a moderate, caring and responsible monarch, who had nothing but the welfare of his subjects at heart. Unfortunately, the message failed to get through. The Jacobites had always been guilty of confusing anti-government sentiment with pro-Jacobite feeling. This was far from being the case; very few individuals of real political or social influence trusted the Pretender or his promises. The Whig propaganda machine easily countered most of James's arguments, and while the committed Jacobites would always follow his lead, those politicians, noblemen and gentry who strongly opposed some aspects of government policy and whom the Jacobites therefore needed to win over to their side, remained firmly in the Hanoverian camp.

Those who did finally rally to the Jacobite standard during the '45 were largely those who had little to lose in terms of prosperity, property or status. In Scotland not a single duke (Perth's title was a Jacobite creation) or marquis (Tullibardine held his title by virtue of being eldest son of the 1st Duke of Atholl) supported Charles. Only three out of over seventy Scottish earls gave their support to the prince: one of these, Alexander, Earl of Kellie, was practically an imbecile, while Earls Kilmarnock and Cromarty were both impoverished. Kilmarnock, indeed, later confessed that 'for the two Kings and their rights, I cared not a farthing which prevailed; but I was starving, and, by God, if Mahommed had set up his standard in the Highlands I had been a good Mussulman for bread, and stuck close to the party, for I must eat'. The Viscounts of Strathallan and Dundee and the Lords Balmerino,

Nairne, Pitsligo, Lovat, Murray and Drummond, together with the eldest sons of the Earls of Airlie and Wemyss (Lords Ogilvy and Elcho respectively) and Lord Lewis Gordon (younger brother of the 3rd Duke of Gordon), made up the bulk of Charles Edward's aristocratic following. With the exception of Lord George Murray, who was appointed sheriff-depute of Perthshire by his brother, Duke James, not one of the above held government posts of any sort at the outbreak of the rising. Believing themselves alienated from the Hanoverian regime, and only too aware of their own financial difficulties, these men were willing recruits to the cause. It was much the same picture for the Jacobite gentry. Many were on the brink of bankruptcy (Murray of Broughton being one), few held office or rank in the civil service or army and none saw any future for themselves or their families while George II remained on the throne.

Many of the Highland chieftains (or their representatives) who joined Charles were also motivated by economic and social considerations. Resentment at the power and influence of Clan Campbell was strong in the western Highlands: the Duke of Argyll had acquired feudal superiority over the lands of a number of the smaller clans, notably the Camerons and the Stewarts of Appin, while the Glencoe Macdonalds' hatred of the Campbells following the Massacre of Glencoe in 1692 was sufficient reason for that small sept to give their support to anyone likely to provide them with the opportunity for revenge. While it is going too far to suggest that these clans rose in favour of Charles Edward purely out of a desire to strike back at Clan Campbell, this was, nevertheless, an important factor in helping the chiefs to decide whether or not to espouse his cause. It is also significant that both Lochiel and Cluny Macpherson pressurised the prince into providing financial security for their lands before undertaking to join him.

Religion also played a part. Not surprisingly, the Catholic Stuarts received backing from their co-religionists, the Glengarry and Clanranald Macdonalds, while the Episcopalian lairds of the north-east Lowlands were also staunch Jacobites. Both groups detested and resented the Presbyterian oligarchy who drew their support from the main Lowland towns of the central belt and from the south-west of the country. James and Charles both advocated religious toleration and promised that there would be no persecution of dissenting sects of whatever denomination. To Episcopalians and Roman Catholics, accustomed to years of prejudice and discrimination, such assurances were sufficient reason for believing that they would be far better off with the Stuarts than with the Hanoverians.

From this it would be easy to infer that those chieftains and Lowland lairds who 'came out' during the '45 did so largely on social, economic or religious grounds and that ideological conviction played little part in determining their actions. This would be hugely unfair to many of the Jacobite leaders — Lord George Murray, the Duke of Perth, Lord Pitsligo, Gordon of Glenbucket and Lord Balmerino, to name but a few — who sincerely believed James to be the rightful king not only of Scotland, but also of Great Britain. Their own somewhat straitened circumstances merely ensured that the decision each took to join the prince was not a difficult one to make. For some of the clan chiefs, however, their natural Jacobitism was mitigated by the desire to safeguard their own interests and position. Some — Macdonald of Sleat and Macleod of Macleod in particular — simply refused to have anything to do with the rising, while others — Lovat, Glengarry and Clanranald being the more obvious examples — sent their sons or other kinsmen to lead the clan while they remained at home. By their very behaviour these chiefs clearly showed that unswerving loyalty to the Stuarts could no longer be guaranteed, particularly if supporting the cause threatened the clan's very existence. Charles was right to target the Highlands as being the only place on mainland Britain where large numbers of men sympathetic to the Stuart cause and accustomed to warfare might be found, but he was shortly to be disabused of the notion that they would all automatically rally to his standard.

2 NEWS FROM MOIDART

*In a state of profound tranquillity, we have been alarmed with advices, which are
said to have been received at London, of intended invasions; and particularly
of a visit which the Pretender's eldest son is about to make to us, if he has
not already made it.*
(DUNCAN FORBES TO HENRY PELHAM, 2 AUGUST 1745)

FROM May onwards events moved rapidly. While staying at the Navarre
residence of his uncle, the Duc de Bouillon, Charles and Sheridan, in a
flurry of activity designed to cover the prince's real aims, sent a series
of letters to King Louis, the Marquis d'Argenson (French Foreign Secretary)
and Daniel O'Brien (James's most trusted confidant) pleading for a renewed
attempt against England. At the same time arms and ammunition, together
with the expedition's war chest, were secretly loaded aboard the *Du Teillay*
which was then at anchor at St Nazaire. Despite the need for secrecy, Charles
was aware that both his father and Louis would eventually have to be informed
of his true intentions. Accordingly he wrote to the two monarchs outlining his
plans, but it was arranged that the letters should arrive at their respective
destinations only after the prince was clear of France.

*Highland dress in the early
eighteenth century. (National
Library of Scotland; on loan
to the Scottish National
Portrait Gallery)*

In his letter to James, Charles began somewhat disingenuously:

I have been, above six months ago, invited by our friends to go to Scotland, and to carry what money and arms I could conveniently get; this being, they are fully persuaded, the only way of restoring you to the Crown, and them to their Liberties…I have tried all possible means and strategies to get access to the King of France, or his Minister, without the least effect…Now I have been obliged to steal off, without letting the King of France so much as suspect it…Let what will happen, the stroke is struck, and I have taken a firm resolution to conquer or to die and stand my ground as long as I shall have a man remaining with me.

The tone of his letter to Louis is conciliatory, but emphasises the need for French assistance:

I have resolved to make myself known by my deeds and on my own to undertake a project which would be certain to succeed with a moderate amount of help. I dare to think that Your Majesty will not refuse it to me…I beg Your Majesty to reflect that in supporting the justice of my claim, you will put yourself in a position to reach a firm and lasting peace, the final conclusion to the war in which you are presently engaged. At last I go to seek my destiny which other than being in the hands of God is in Your Majesty's.

The letters, both dated 12 June, would seem to suggest that whatever suspicions James and Louis may have harboured regarding the prince's intentions, neither monarch had really been aware of the full extent of his plans. The letters also demonstrate that Charles appreciated just how necessary French support was for the venture to succeed. In June 1745 there was absolutely no guarantee that this support would be forthcoming, and it is difficult to avoid concluding that Charles, in his quest for personal glory, was prepared to risk the lives and fortunes of others on the off-chance that Louis XV would change his mind. If for no other reason, recent personal experience should have warned the prince against trusting the French court.

With the letters safely dispatched, the prince's party then made their way in various disguises under assumed names and by different routes to Nantes, where they met up again as if by chance. They then sailed down the Loire, arriving in the evening at St Nazaire where they spent the night at an inn. Charles, whose true identity was to be kept from the crew of the *Du Teillay*, was persuaded by Walsh to alter his disguise from that of a student at the Scots College in Paris to one of an Irish priest. The next morning, 22 June, the prince and his entourage boarded the *Du Teillay*, commanded by Captain Darbé, and, after a delay caused by contrary winds, set sail for Belle-Isle.

The *Du Teillay* was obliged to wait until 2 July for the *Elisabeth*, commanded by Captain D'Au, to join her. On board the *Elisabeth* were some 1500 firearms, 1800 broadswords, twenty small cannon and a contingent of about 100 men from Clare's regiment, who would provide a useful escort for the prince once he landed in Scotland. On 4 July the two ships set sail at 5 a.m. and proceeded in a north-westerly direction. Although they encountered a number of ships, Darbé believed them to be from Brest and the expedition continued on its way without interference. On Tuesday 9 July, however, their luck changed.

Darbé recorded events in the *Du Teillay*'s log:

> We heard several shots fired coming from the N.E. We perceived that they were pursuing us, and coming obliquely upon us. Seeing the said ships nearing us we spoke M. D'au, commander of the Elisabeth, and prepared for battle at noon. The sail vessel was to the E. at a distance of a league and a half with all sails set to overtake us. We recognised it as a ship with two and a half batteries, suspected to be English.

The English ship was in fact the *Lion,* a 60-gun man-of-war commanded by Captain Percy Brett. In its July edition the *Scots Magazine* carried a report of the encounter which followed:

> On the 9th of July, the Lion, of 58 guns, Capt. Brett, being in lat. 47.57. N. and West from the meridian of the Lizard 39 Leagues, bore down upon two French men of war, one of 64 guns, the other of 16. At 5 o'clock the Lion ran along-side the large ship, and began to engage within pistol-shot, and continued in that situation till 10; during which time they kept a continual fire at each other; when, the Lion's rigging being cut to pieces…all her lower masts and top masts shot through in many places, so that she lay muzzled in the sea, and could do nothing with her sails, the French ship sheered off, and in less than an hour was out of sight, the Lion not being able to follow her. The small ship, in the beginning of the engagement, made two attempts to rake the Lion; but was soon beat off by her stern-chase, and after that lay off at a great distance. The Lion had 45 men killed outright, and 107 wounded, 7 of whom died of their wounds soon after.

But if the *Lion* had suffered badly, so too had the *Elisabeth*. Although she had won the bruising encounter on points, 140 of her crew — including Captain D'Au — were killed, and 160 wounded. Altogether over 450 men had either lost their lives or been injured in this first engagement of the '45; it was a bloody beginning to the campaign. Moreover, as a result of the serious damage she had sustained, it was clear that the *Elisabeth* would now never reach Scotland, nor could she risk coming alongside the *Du Teillay* to transfer the troops, arms and ammunition she was carrying, in case she capsized. The decision was quickly made; the *Elisabeth* must return to Brest for repairs, leaving the *Du Teillay* to continue the voyage alone.

It is not difficult to imagine the prevailing mood on board the *Du Teillay* once the *Elisabeth* departed. Deprived of the protection offered by the larger ship, Darbé and Walsh now had to rely on speed, subterfuge and, above all, luck, if they were to get to Scotland without further disaster befalling them. During the week following the sea-fight several more ships were sighted, including two which seemed to take more than a passing interest in the

movements of the frigate. Fortunately a storm blew up, allowing the *Du Teillay* to make her escape. Then, at 4 a.m. on Saturday 20 July, Darbé sighted land. Regrettably it was not South Uist as the captain had hoped, but the north coast of Ireland. No land was sighted the next day and Darbé admitted that the route he had taken was 'not promising'.

But morale improved the following day when the crew sighted Barra Head on the island of Berneray, the southernmost point of the Outer Hebrides. Darbé steered towards Barra, bringing the *Du Teillay* alongside the island, and Aeneas Macdonald and Duncan Cameron were put ashore in the ship's boat to see if they could find a local pilot willing to guide them through the treacherous waters off the north-west coast of Scotland. Shortly after this, Walsh intercepted a boat coming over from the mainland carrying 'a horse, a calf, a woman, and children' and took the master aboard in order that he too might act as pilot. Macdonald and Cameron soon returned, bringing one Calum McNeil, the Laird of Barra's piper, with them. Now adequately provided with pilots, the *Du Teillay* made for the island of Canna, but they were forced to abandon this plan on the appearance of a large ship which Darbé assumed was a British man-of-war. The *Du Teillay* immediately altered course to search for a suitable haven between Barra and South Uist offering the possibility, if required, of escape to the west.

Darbé's fears were realised when, on changing direction, the English ship also altered course and pursued them. Believing that his passengers might be captured or killed if the man-of-war caught up, Walsh had them embark on the ship's boat and set them ashore on Eriskay. On 23 July Charles Edward Stuart, in somewhat ignominious circumstances, set foot on Scottish soil for the first time. That night, in appalling weather, the prince and his companions rested in the house of Angus Macdonald, a local crofter. Fortunately the strong winds prevented the English ship from entering the harbour and she was forced to put into another haven about a mile away from where the *Du Teillay* was anchored.

If the situation the prince found himself in seemed far from promising that evening, matters took a turn for the worse early next morning when Alexander Macdonald of Boisdale, brother of Clanranald, visited him. Boisdale refused to join him and begged the prince to return to France and await a more favourable opportunity. Moreover, he informed Charles that neither Sir Alexander Macdonald of Sleat nor Macleod of Macleod would have anything to do with him unless he was supported by French troops. This was a devastating blow: Charles had been depending on support from the two powerful Skye chieftains who, between them, could have put 2000 men into the field. O'Sullivan was probably not exaggerating when he said that, on hearing Boisdale, 'Every body was strock as with a thunder boult, as you may believe, to hear yt sentence'. (Charles was not to know that both men were effectively being blackmailed into staying 'loyal' to the government. In 1740 Macdonald and Macleod had forcibly kidnapped almost one hundred of their tenants in an attempt to sell them to an Irish shipowner bound for the colonies of North America. Duncan Forbes of Culloden, Lord President of the Court of Session, exercised his discretion and never brought charges against the two men. In return for his co-operation however, there seems little doubt that Forbes extracted guarantees from both chiefs that neither would participate in any future Jacobite rising.) Most of Charles's companions, with the exception of Walsh and possibly O'Sullivan, then urged the prince to abandon the attempt and return to France. Charles would have none of this, insisting that renewed efforts be made to persuade Macleod and Sleat to reconsider, and a messenger was subsequently dispatched with the prince's instructions.

At 8 a.m. Darbé sent a boat to pick up the prince's entourage, Boisdale also coming aboard, where he engaged in further debate with Charles. Nor was there any respite from the British navy. By 9 a.m. the man-of-war had reappeared, this time accompanied by a frigate, and was making repeated efforts to tack into the harbour. Only contrary winds prevented her from achieving this, and it was decided that the only hope of escape lay in sailing away that evening under cover of darkness. Almost for the first time since he had left France, luck was with the prince that night, and the *Du Teillay* made good her escape. Darbé described the voyage:

> I arrived between Scaye and Canay and continued my course eastward, not wishing to anchor at the said islands for fear those vessels should come to seek for us there. When I had passed Rum and Canay, Eigg was on my

starboard and the mainland in front of us. I continued my course to find it…I saw to eastward of my port a low point jutting out from the mainland, and beyond the point a rock in the form of an island…Mr Macdonald embarked in a boat we had brought from Barra, with his servant, to go and find a brother who was in this country. I steered east and anchored at 3 o'clock in the evening [25 July] at the head of a bay, a fine plain with a few poor houses and a great many cattle. The place is called Lochnanuagh [Loch nan Uamh]. At 4 o'clock I lowered my boat and…the Prince with three or four gentlemen landed and went to the houses.

In the days which followed the landing, representatives of the various branches of Clan Donald came to pay their respects to the prince. Their support was crucial, but despite protestations of loyalty and devotion, the overwhelming opinion of the visitors was that Charles should go back to France and not return unless accompanied by French troops. Displaying characteristic Stuart disregard for sound advice, Charles insisted on going ahead with his plans. Kinlochmoidart was sent to summon Murray of Broughton, the Duke of Perth and young Lochiel, while Ranald Macdonald, 'young Clanranald', set out for Skye in a further attempt to change the minds of Sleat and Macleod. At about this time there came aboard the *Du Teillay* a young Clanranald Macdonald (almost certainly the famous Gaelic bard, Alasdair Mac Mhaighstir Alasdair) who was later to write an account of the rising, and it is from him that we get our first description of Charles at this critical stage of proceedings. Going on board they found that a large tent had been erected on deck which was 'well furnished with wines and spirits'. Clanranald went below deck to speak with Charles; some time later he returned and joined his companions on deck where they were entertained by Tullibardine. An hour and a half later Charles made his appearance:

> There entered the tent a tall youth of a most agreeable aspect in a plain black coat with a plain shirt not very clean and a cambrick stock fixed with a plain silver buckle, a fair round wig out of the buckle, a plain hatt with a canvas string haveing one end fixed to one of his coat buttons; he had black stockins and brass buckles in his shoes; at his first appearance I found my heart swell to my very throat. We were immediately told by one Obrian a churchman that this youth was also ane English clergyman who had long been possess'd with a desire to see and converse with Highlanders.

Clearly the writer was not fooled by the disguise, and his account of the prince's behaviour during their meeting indicates that Charles was in good humour despite all the recent disappointments. A further setback arose, however, when young Clanranald returned to confirm that neither Skye chieftain was prepared to reconsider his position. With this, even Walsh advised the prince to leave, and the future of the rising hung by a frayed thread. In a final, desperate appeal for support, Charles turned to Ranald Macdonald, brother of Kinlochmoidart, and asked the young man if he would not assist his rightful prince. 'I will,' Ranald replied, 'though no other man in the Highlands should draw his sword.' Charles's ploy worked. Shamed by his kinsman's reply, young Clanranald agreed to raise his clan and, in case no other chief joined, 'to guard the person of the Prince against his enemies for 6 months at least'. Clanranald's decision had the desired effect: those representatives of the other Macdonald clans present, notably Keppoch and Glencoe, agreed to do likewise, and Charles had the beginnings of an army.

This initial success was followed by a far more significant achievement — the wooing of Lochiel. Donald Cameron, younger of Lochiel, was the eldest son of John, 18th chief of Clan Cameron (then in exile in France) and his father's representative. As acting head of the most powerful Lochaber clan, Lochiel's support was vital: not only was he able to put almost 1000 men in the field, but such was his influence that others would undoubtedly follow his lead. However, in late July 1745, the omens were not good. Like Murray of Broughton, and others, Lochiel believed that if a rising were to take place without the backing of French troops then it was bound to end in failure. His loyalty to the House of Stuart was never in any doubt, but his devotion was tempered by pragmatism.

At first Lochiel refused to obey his prince's summons, sending instead his brother, Dr Archibald Cameron, to persuade Charles to abandon his enterprise. Charles refused to accept this, and sent a further summons to Lochiel inviting him to 'do his duty'. Reluctantly Lochiel complied and made his way north where he encountered another of his brothers, John Cameron of Fassifern, who advised him to avoid Charles, for 'if this Prince once sets his eyes upon you he will make you do whatever he pleases'. Fassifern's warning was prophetic. It is not entirely clear just how Charles persuaded the reluctant Lochiel to change his mind, but persuade him he did, albeit at the cost of guaranteeing financial compensation to the full value of Lochiel's estates should the campaign prove unsuccessful. Lochiel also insisted that Macdonald of Glengarry give a written assurance that he would raise his clan for the prince — a guarantee which was provided by Glengarry's son, Angus. Charles had paid a high price, but it was one well worth paying; now, at last, the clans were rallying.

The clan representatives departed to raise their men — Charles giving each a sum of money to help encourage recruitment — and agreed to assemble on 19 August at Glenfinnan, where Charles would raise his father's royal standard. On Monday 29 July the *Du Teillay* had set sail for Loch Ailort to the south of Loch nan Uamh, where she anchored, and the crew began to unload a quantity of arms, ammunition and other stores. On Wednesday 7 August, Darbé and Walsh went ashore for the last time to take their leave of Charles and his companions. It must have been an emotional farewell: Charles was fully aware of the vital part the Irishman had played in getting him to Scotland, an awareness reflected in the prince's decision to bestow a knighthood on Walsh and present him with a gold-hilted sword. After taking aboard oxen and sheep for provisions, the *Du Teillay* finally departed,

Donald Cameron of Lochiel, 19th chief of Clan Cameron (1695?-1748). Donald Cameron was known as the 'gentle' Lochiel by comparison with his formidable grandfather, Ewen. After overcoming his initial reluctance, Lochiel was perhaps the staunchest supporter Charles had among his colonels, and, like most of them, he was prepared to burn the homes of his clansmen to bring them 'out' in rebellion. This portrait was painted some years after his death. (By kind permission of Sir Donald Cameron of Lochiel, KT)

British grenadiers. In the late 1740s, the Duke of Cumberland commissioned the French artist David Morier to depict the uniforms of the regiments which had served under him. (The Royal Collection© Her Majesty Queen Elizabeth II)

leaving Charles alone with a few companions and a small guard of Highlanders provided by Clanranald.

A few days after the departure of the *Du Teillay*, Charles left Borrodale and set out for Kinlochmoidart. The prince travelled by sea around the headlands of Loch nan Uamh and Loch Ailort while his Clanranald guard marched along the shore. Charles stayed at Kinlochmoidart until 17 August and made preparations for the heavy baggage to be sent on to Glenfinnan. While he remained there the first military encounters of the rising took place. On 14 August Captain Sweetenham of Guise's regiment — 'an English Officer, & a piece of an Ingenier' — on his way from Ruthven Barracks to repair the fortifications at Fort William, was captured by a number of Keppoch's men, thereby earning the dubious distinction of becoming the first prisoner of the '45. It was not long before he was joined by others. On 16 August two recently formed companies of the Royal Scots, numbering some sixty officers and men, were making their way to Fort William along the shores of Loch Lochy. As they approached High Bridge they were ambushed by twelve of Keppoch's men commanded by Macdonald of Tirnadris. This was guerilla warfare — Highland style — at its best. The Macdonalds kept on the move, firing at the soldiers from behind trees and rocks, never allowing the Royal Scots to settle and return fire. Whenever the clansmen were forced to break cover they huddled together, holding their kilts out wide so as to create the impression of greater numbers. Forced to back away, the regular troops had to endure being sniped at by an unseen enemy for some three miles before Tirnadris was joined by more of Keppoch's men and a detachment of Lochiel's Camerons at Laggan, at the head of the loch. On seeing these reinforcements, Captain Scott, who commanded the government

A map of the central Highlands prepared for intelligence purposes, showing the number of men each clan chief could raise. (National Library of Scotland, Z3/41 a&b)

troops, gave the order to surrender. Two or three of his men had been killed and a number more wounded, including Scott himself. Although not significant in terms of numbers involved, the skirmish at High Bridge greatly encouraged the traditionally superstitious Highlanders who regarded it as a favourable portent of things to come.

On 18 August, having been joined by John Murray of Broughton, Charles left Kinlochmoidart and went to Glenaladale, where he was met by John Gordon of Glenbucket and the unfortunate Captain Sweetenham. At 7 a.m. the next morning the prince, escorted by about fifty of Clanranald's clan, set out for Glenfinnan at the head of Loch Shiel. He arrived there at 1 p.m. and was met by another Clanranald contingent numbering some 150 men: of the other clans, however, there was no sign. The sight of the empty, lonely glen must have filled Charles with dread; had the chiefs reconsidered and decided that the risks were too great? Two long, nerve-racking hours later, the distant echo of the pipes was heard in the glen. As the sound grew louder, anxious eyes scanned the surrounding hills, hoping for a first sight of the advancing pipers. In a moment of unbearable tension and drama, a dark mass appeared moving down the hillside — Clan Cameron had arrived. With Lochiel at their head the 800 clansmen (many of whom were reluctant recruits forced out by their chief) advanced in two columns to where a greatly relieved Charles Edward Stuart welcomed them. Lochiel's arrival meant that the ceremony could now begin. The following account was written either by young Clanranald himself or, more probably, by one of his kinsmen:

Glenfinnan at the head of Loch Shiel. The monument was erected in the nineteenth century. (National Trust for Scotland)

> The Royal Standard was displayed in the following manner, viz. as soon as the D. of Athole crossed the River [Finnan], he gave the Standard into the P[rince]'s hand who returnd it back to him with orders to display it wch the Duke did standing in the middle of the Mcdonalds, and immediately the King's and Prince's declarations were read. After this all the highlanders threw their bonnets in the air and huzza'd 3 different times, crying alowd long live K. James the 8, and Charles P. of Wales, prosperity to Scotld and no union. When this ceremony was over, the D. returned with the Standard to HRH's quarters…About 6 of clock in the evening Mcdonald of Keppoch arrivd with 350 men carrying along with them two companys of Guise's Regiment, whom he had taken two days before at High Bridge as they were on their march to Fort Wm. About the same time Stuart of Innerhayle came from Appin to aquaint the P. that his men would join him in a few days.

After the formalities were completed, Charles ordered some casks of brandy to be distributed to the men so that they could drink the King's health. It was observed by a number of those present 'that at no other time did [Charles] look more cheerful or display a greater buoyancy of spirits' than he did while at Glenfinnan. This was hardly surprising: three weeks earlier barely a man in the Highlands seemed willing to join him, now, largely through the force of his own personality and his dogged refusal to listen to the advice of the very men whose lives and property would be most at risk, he had some 1200 men under arms.

It was a notable achievement. But could this little army now restore a king to his throne?

*****

That the government in London did nothing to prevent Charles Edward Stuart from raising an army in the Highlands of Scotland — an army whose sole purpose was to overthrow the very regime they represented — may seem incredible to the modern reader. But that is to ignore one simple fact: no government can act, even to protect itself, without adequate intelligence. The prince, after all, had landed in one of mainland Britain's most remote areas, an area almost inaccessible to outsiders and inhabited by a people still loyal to the House of Stuart. It was hardly surprising, therefore, that in the days immediately following the prince's landing, there was very little — if any — 'news from Moidart'.

But reports of a renewed effort to restore the Stuarts did eventually reach the government. On 1 August the Duke of Newcastle, Secretary of State for the Southern Department, wrote to the Duke of Argyll informing him that George II, then in Hanover, had received 'undoubted intelligence, that the resolution was actually taken at the court of France, to attempt immediately an invasion of his Majesty's British Dominions'. Apparently, continued Newcastle, the Dutch ambassador had sent a message to his government informing them that 'the Pretender's eldest son embarked on the 15th of July, at Nantes, on board a ship of about sixty guns, attended by a frigate, loaded with arms for a considerable number of men; and that it was universally believed, that they were gone for Scotland.' The Dutch ambassador's account was received by the Lords Justices on 30 July and the Scottish Secretary, John Hay, Marquis of Tweeddale, then sent instructions to Lieutenant-General Sir John Cope, Commander in Chief of the Forces in Scotland, to 'assemble the troops in proper places, and to order the dragoon horses to be taken up from grass'. These instructions arrived at Edinburgh on Friday 2 August.

As a result of this intelligence, the *London Gazette* of 3 August published a proclamation ordering 'a reward of thirty thousand pounds to any person who shall seize and secure the eldest son of the Pretender; in case he shall land, or attempt to land, in any of his Majesty's dominions'. In order to encourage any of those who might already have joined Charles to betray him, the proclamation concluded: 'And, if any of the persons who have adhered to or assisted, or who shall adhere to or assist the said pretender, or his said son, shall seize and secure him the said son as aforesaid, he or they who shall so seize and secure him, shall have his Majesty's gracious pardon, and shall also receive the said award.' It is a measure of the Highlanders' loyalty to their prince that not one of them sought to take advantage of the government's offer.

John Hay, 4th Marquess of Tweeddale (d.1762), by William Aikman. When Tweeddale's handling of the crisis caused by the outbreak of rebellion led to his resignation as Secretary of State for Scotland in January 1746, the office lapsed. It was only revived in the nineteenth century. (Scottish National Portrait Gallery)

The real problem facing the government at this stage, however, was that hardly anyone took the threat seriously. On being informed of Tweeddale's instructions to Cope, the Lord President of the Court of Session, Duncan Forbes of Culloden, admitted to Henry Pelham, the First Lord of the Treasury and Newcastle's brother, that 'these informations…I must confess, have not hitherto gain'd my belief'. Despite his reservations, Forbes decided to travel north to his estates 'a little earlier than usual' in order to 'give some countenance to the friends of the government, and prevent the seduction of the unwary, if there should be any truth in what is reported'. This scepticism was shared by Tweeddale who, as late as 17 August — long after the government had received irrefutable evidence of the prince's arrival — wrote, 'I owe I have never been alarmed with the Reports of the Pretender's Son landing in Scotland. I consider it as a rash and desperate attempt, that can have no other consequence than the ruin of those concerned in it.'

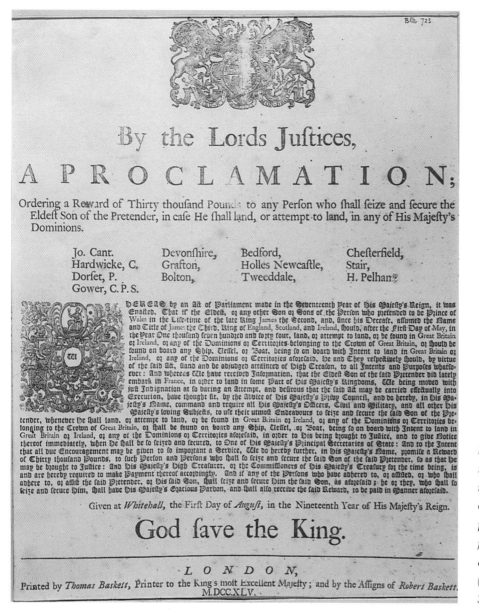

Proclamation of a reward of £30,000 (approximately £2.4 million today) for the capture of Prince Charles. When the prince heard about this he jokingly offered £30 for the capture of George II. (National Library of Scotland, Blk.723)

When news from Moidart finally did arrive, it merely served to confirm what the government already knew. The information was provided by the Reverend Lauchlan Campbell, minister at Ardnamurchan. Upon observing that 'all my Jacobites were in high spirits', he made enquiries as to the identities of the occupants of a ship which had lately 'put in to Lochnanua in Arisaig where no man alive saw ship drop anchor before that time'. One of his parishioners, Anna Cameron, 'a great Whig', confirmed that the prince had indeed arrived in the minister's parish. Campbell duly passed on this news, via the Duke of Argyll's factor and the sheriff-depute of Argyll, to Lord Milton, the Lord Justice Clerk, then staying at Rosneath with the duke. Milton forwarded the information to Cope in Edinburgh where it arrived on 8 August. The following day, Forbes called on Cope 'in his boots' on his way north to Culloden. Forbes had received further confirmation that morning of

the prince's landing. His informant was none other than Macleod of Macleod, who had written to Forbes on 3 August following young Clanranald's unsuccessful mission to Skye on Charles's behalf. Macleod assured Forbes that both he and Macdonald of Sleat 'gave no sort of Countenance to these people, but we used all the interest we had with our Neighbours to follow the same prudent method'.

Meantime, in the midst of ever increasing speculation as to the whereabouts and intentions of the prince, Cope organised the military response. It was no simple matter: his forces were scattered throughout the length and breadth of Scotland, and he sent orders for the various units to assemble at Stirling, from where they would march to Fort Augustus and engage the rebels immediately, 'as it was the most probable Method of disconcerting the Designs of the Enemies to his Majesty's government'. Every effort was made to speed up preparations: 'The Ovens at Leith, Stirling and Perth, were kept at Work Day and Night, Sunday not excepted, to provide Biscuit.' But, despite all his efforts, Cope was delayed at Edinburgh for longer than he would have wished owing to the shortage of provisions, as well as by a lack of money 'wherewith to subsist the Troops'. Finally, however, all was ready, and on 19 August the *Caledonian Mercury* reported, 'This Forenoon his Excellency Sir John Cope, Commander in Chief of the Forces in Scotland, set out for Stirling, accompanied by the Right Hon. the Earl of Lowdon, and a great many other military Officers, in order to put himself at the Head of the Army.'

As Cope began his march north from Edinburgh, Charles Edward Stuart was arriving at Glenfinnan: a clash of arms now appeared inevitable.

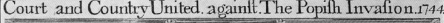

3 SOUTH TO EDINBURGH

It is to be observed, that the City of Edr. is surrounded with a good old Wall, wch cannot be forced, but with cannon; & it is reasonable to suppose, that it cannot be surprised when guarded by such a number of Men. There is already one compleat Regt. of Dragoons.
(MEMORANDUM FROM THE EARL OF STAIR TO THE MINISTRY, AUGUST 1745)

Affairs in this City and Neighbourhood have taken the most surprizing Turn since Yesterday, without the least Bloodshed or Opposition; so that now we have in our Streets Highlanders and Bagpipes, in place of Dragoons and Drums.
(CALEDONIAN MERCURY, 18 SEPTEMBER 1745)

CHARLES remained at Glenfinnan for two days distributing such arms as he had to the clansmen before setting out for Kinlocheil on 21 August. At this early stage in the campaign there is little to suggest that the prince had any definite strategy in mind other than augmenting his rather inadequate army and, if circumstances allowed, bringing Cope to battle as quickly as possible. Charles had obviously learned much from the 1715 rising, when the dilatory and vacillating Earl of Mar surrendered the initiative to his opposite number on the Hanoverian side, John, 2nd Duke of Argyll. In squandering the undoubted advantages the Jacobites then possessed through his unwillingness to engage Argyll's much smaller army at the earliest opportunity, Mar was largely responsible for the rising's failure. Charles Edward did not intend to make the same mistake.

And for a few days it seemed as if Sir John Cope would do his best to oblige the prince. Cope's instructions from Tweeddale were perfectly clear: he was to seek out and destroy the rebels before they could march south and

Ewan Macpherson of Cluny to Lord President Duncan Forbes, 18 August 1745. The postscript mentions rumours about the raising of the prince's standard at Glenfinnan. Like a number of other officers in the government's independent companies, Macpherson later defected to the Stuart cause. (National Library of Scotland, MS.2969, ff.11-12 r.&v.)

The Prince's route from Moidart to Edinburgh.

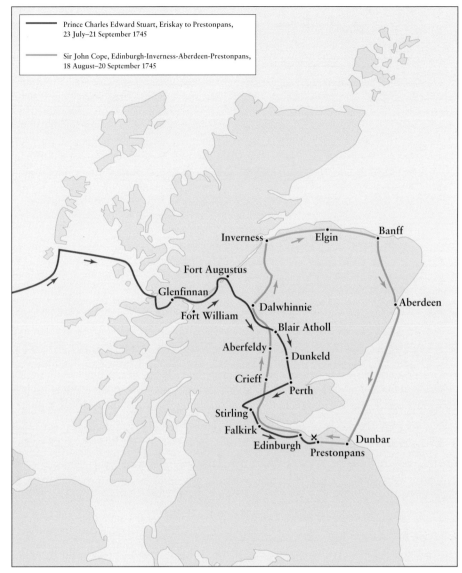

Prince Charles Edward Stuart, Eriskay to Prestonpans,
23 July–21 September 1745

Sir John Cope, Edinburgh-Inverness-Aberdeen-Prestonpans,
18 August–20 September 1745

Banff

Inverness   Elgin

Fort Augustus

Glenfinnan   Dalwhinnie   Aberdeen

Fort William   Blair Atholl

Aberfeldy   Dunkeld

Crieff

Perth

Stirling

Falkirk   Dunbar

Edinburgh   Prestonpans

John Erskine, 6th Earl of Mar (1675-1732), with his son Thomas, Lord Erskine. Mar had been willing to serve King George I on his accession in 1714, but the following year he raised a rebellion in the Highlands in favour of the Stuarts after the king pointedly turned his back on him at a court reception. (National Library of Scotland; on loan to the Scottish National Portrait Gallery)

before they could be reinforced by other pro-Jacobite clans. Cope was poorly equipped to carry out these instructions: his army could not have numbered more than 1800 men at this time, most of whom — particularly the newly recruited companies of the Earl of Loudoun's Highland regiment — were inadequately trained and untested in battle. Nevertheless, he set out from Stirling on 20 August intending to make his way to the 'Chain' (the name given by government soldiers to Wade's road leading from Inverness to Fort William). The army was accompanied by a herd of black cattle, numbers of which were slaughtered at regular intervals to provide fresh meat for the troops, without which, according to one officer, 'we would have starved upon the march'. The government army's progress was further hampered by the fact they had to carry with them over 1000 stand of arms for a 'body of the well-affected Highlanders' who were to join with them at Crieff. Much to Cope's disgust, if not to his surprise, not a single 'loyal' Highlander was to be found at that town on their arrival. Anticipating correctly that he was now

THE

Edinburgh Evening Courant.

NUM. 7709.

MONDAY, DECEMBER 23. 1745.

From the London Gazette, Dec. 17.

Petersbourg, November 16.

... ER Imperial Majesty has nominated M. Ne-

count that is to be got here of the Engagement, is taken from what his Pruffian Majefty has written about it under his own Hand, the Subftance of which is, That the Army under the King himfelf, marched from Konigsbruck to Meiffen; the reigning Prince of Anhalt, reinfo... ed by a

Num. 3901

The Caledonian Mercury.

Edinburgh, Monday, October 14, 1745.

EDINBURGH, Oct. 14.

CHARLES P.R.

...HARLES Prince of Wales, &c. Regent of the

ons, the King cannot poffibly ratify it, fince he has had repeated Remonftrances againft it from each Kingdom; and fince it is inconteftable, that the principal Point then

The Courant *and the* Mercury *were carried by post all over Scotland. Allegations of partisanship were levelled at both publications, particularly during the Jacobite occupation of Edinburgh when the* Courant *adopted a sullenly neutral approach to events, while the* Mercury *triumphantly carried a series of blatantly pro-Jacobite editorials. (National Library of Scotland)*

unlikely to be reinforced, Cope sent over 700 of these arms back to Stirling Castle in order to facilitate his march over the difficult terrain which lay ahead. Continuing northwards through Aberfeldy, Trinifuir and Dalnacardoch, Cope reached Dalwhinnie on 26 August. Here he received intelligence (from Duncan Forbes among others) that the Highland army was waiting for them at the Pass of Corrieyairack. The news unsettled those officers who knew the area well; here was ideal country — a steep, narrow route flanked by mountains and concealed hollows — for the lightly armed and mobile clansmen to ambush the far more cumbersome government forces.

Cope was not to know that on 26 August Charles was in fact at Invergarry, and therefore not immediately in a position to oppose the Hanoverians at Corrieyairack. This lack of reliable, accurate intelligence was to plague commanders on both sides during the rising and, ultimately, was to have a profound effect in determining the outcome of the '45. The prince had reached Invergarry, having marched from Kinlocheil by way of Fassifern, Moy and Letterfinlay. On his march Charles obtained a copy of the Lords Justices' proclamation offering £30,000 for his capture, which he dismissed lightheartedly, proposing in return a reward of £30 for the head of George II. During his stay at Invergarry, Charles was joined by some 250 Stewarts of Appin, commanded by Stewart of Ardshiel, and received his first communication from Simon Fraser, Lord Lovat.

As an inveterate intriguer and self-seeking schemer, Lovat was without peer anywhere in Scotland. Unwilling to commit himself to either side until he was sure of the outcome, Lovat constructed a series of fences on which he

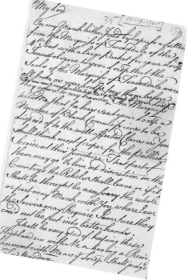

Sir John Cope, commander-in-chief in Scotland, to Duncan Forbes, undated. Cope kept the civil authorities informed of his movements and intentions on his ill-met expedition through the central Highlands in August and September 1745. (National Library of Scotland, MS. 2969, f.15a)

The town of Inverness, from John Slezer's Theatrum Scotiae *of 1693. (National Library of Scotland)*

Simon Fraser, 11th Lord Lovat (c1667-1747), by William Hogarth. It was only after the Jacobite victory at Prestonpans that Lovat sent Clan Fraser, commanded by his son, to join Charles Edward. Captured after Culloden, Lovat was eventually executed at Tower Hill in 1747, a victim of his own duplicity and poor judgment. (National Library of Scotland; on loan to the Scottish National Portrait Gallery)

perched precariously during the early stages of the campaign. On 23 August he had written to the Lord Advocate, Robert Craigie, referring to the prince as 'that Mad and unaccountable Gentleman' while at the same time, in the letter Charles received at Invergarry, assuring the prince of his loyalty to the House of Stuart. Lovat apologised to Charles for his men not being in readiness to join him, due, so he said, to the close proximity of government garrisons at Inverness and Fort William, but pledged to join Charles on receipt of the commissions of lieutenant-general and lord lieutenant which had previously been promised him by James. As further proof of his duplicity, as well as in recognition of the threat posed by Forbes both to himself and Charles, Lovat demanded that the prince issue a warrant authorising him to take Duncan Forbes (with whom Lovat was in regular correspondence) 'dead or alive'. Murray of Broughton accordingly issued Lovat with a commission as lieutenant-general as well as with a somewhat modified warrant authorising him to apprehend Forbes and 'keep him in safe custody until further orders'.

The old fox did offer one piece of sound advice, however, in advising Charles to march north through Fraser country where his presence would not only persuade Clan Fraser to rise, but would also encourage the pro-Jacobite Mackenzies, Grants, Macleans and Mackintoshes to come out in support of the prince. Despite the obvious attractions contained in Lovat's proposals, Charles rejected them, as he had just received news of Cope's intentions to seize the Pass of Corrieyairack. The prince hurriedly moved his army northwards to Aberchalder where, on 27 August, he was further reinforced by 400 Glengarry Macdonalds, 120 of Glencoe's men and some Grants of Glenmoriston. Making full use of Wade's famous military roads, the Jacobites then headed south in order to seize the high ground of the pass before Cope arrived, expecting to engage the government army at about noon on the 28th. Murray of Broughton (whom the prince had made his secretary three days earlier) in company with Macdonald of Lochgarry, rode out in advance of the main body to reconnoitre the enemy's disposition. But, to their great surprise, on reaching the top of the pass 'not a Creature was to be seen' except some Highland deserters from Cope's army who informed Lochgarry that Cope had turned his army around and headed for Ruthven in Badenoch.

The reasons behind Cope's disappearing act were explained by one of his officers — later captured at Prestonpans — whose account of events was published in the October issue of the *Gentleman's Magazine*:

> At *Del-whinny* we were informed that the rebels were posted on and in *Corryerrick*, a noted pass, 17 miles distant on our way to the Chain. The General thereupon called together the commanding officers of the several corps, and laid before them the orders he had to march directly to the Chain, and his intelligence about the disposition of the rebels, desiring to have their opinion what was proper to be done…Formerly several of these officers had marched over that ground, and all of them unanimously agreed, that to force the rebels in it was utterly impracticable. It must inevitably be attended with the loss of all our provisions, artillery, military stores &c. and indeed of the troops: that giving the rebels any success upon their first setting out, was by all means to be prevented, as what might be attended with bad consequences to the service.

If they were not to proceed through Corrieyairack, then Cope's council of war was faced with three possible alternatives: to remain where they were and block the Highlanders' march south; retreat to Stirling and prevent Charles from entering Lowland Scotland or, finally, march north to pro-Hanoverian Inverness and from there on to Aberdeen where the army would be able to procure shipping to transport them to Edinburgh. Once again the decision was unanimous. The superior speed and mobility of the Highlanders meant that they would certainly reach Stirling before the slower government troops could get there, and this same speed of movement would also allow them to bypass the Hanoverians 'by roads over the mountains, practicable for them, utterly impracticable for regular troops' should Cope decide to remain at Dalwhinnie. Given that the government soldiers 'had not above two days bread left that could be eat' and that they were 'in a country that could not supply us', the decision to march for Inverness was the only sensible option remaining to Cope. The general was also aware of the devastating effect that a retreat to Stirling might occasion; not only would it damage his own troops' morale, but it might also persuade any number of putative Jacobites to abandon their neutrality and unite behind Charles Edward.

Cope's decision to avoid an early confrontation with the Jacobites has often been interpreted as being militarily unsound. Yet the fault does not lie with Cope but with his political masters in London who insisted that he engage the rebels and crush them at the earliest opportunity. None of these men — including the Scottish Secretary Tweeddale — appreciated the

Duncan Forbes of Culloden (1685-1747). As Lord President of the Court of Session, Forbes used a mixture of persuasion, cajolery and bribery to keep as many as possible of the Highland chiefs loyal to the government. (National Library of Scotland; on loan to the Scottish National Portrait Gallery)

The Porteous Mob by James Drummond, painted in 1855. (National Gallery of Scotland)

difficulties that regular troops, accustomed as they were to rigid regimentation and ponderous drill, would encounter in inhospitable terrain when faced by a much more mobile enemy who were completely at home in their surroundings. In avoiding the Jacobites at Corrieyairack, Cope ensured that his army would live to fight another day. Moreover, the flat plains of the Lowlands would be more conducive to the type of warfare that his officers were used to, and Cope would be able to keep his forces regularly supplied and his lines of communication to the south open.

However, by choosing to march on Inverness, Cope had opened the road to Edinburgh. The Jacobites seized the opportunity and headed south, secure in the knowledge that they would be unlikely to face any serious opposition before reaching the capital. That Scotland was now at the prince's mercy would not have come as a surprise to anyone with more than a passing interest in Scottish affairs. At the start of the rising there were fewer than 4000 government troops stationed in Scotland, half of whom were now marching directly away from the very insurgents they were employed to disperse. Those government forces not with Cope included two regiments of dragoons commanded by Colonels Gardiner and Hamilton which together numbered fewer than 600 troopers. Recently recruited in Ireland, the dragoons, in common with other troops under Cope's overall command, had never seen action and were poorly trained. Cope had left Gardiner's squadrons at Stirling in order to contest any attempt by the Jacobites to cross the Firth of Forth, while Hamilton's men were posted in and around Edinburgh. Most of the remaining government forces were garrisoned at the various forts and castles located throughout Scotland, where their presence was designed either to intimidate those Highland clans whose loyalty to the House of Hanover was suspect, or to support the civilian authorities whenever the local Lowland citizenry attempted to take the law into their own hands — the Glasgow Malt Tax disturbances in 1725 and the Porteous Riot of 1736 in Edinburgh being good examples of the latter. But, once the rebellion had broken out, the forts could be avoided by the Jacobite forces, and while the garrisons might still provide a threat to the prince's lines of communication, the troops stationed there could do little to hinder the Highlanders on their march south.

Not all the Highland clans were disaffected, however, and the government was entitled to believe that a number would actively oppose the Jacobites should a rising take place. But this was to overlook a number of crucial factors which affected the Whig clans' ability to respond during a crisis. The Disarming Acts of 1716 and 1725 sought to ensure that the Jacobite clans would be unable to participate in any future risings by forcing the clansmen to surrender their arms to the government. Unfortunately, the Acts did not distinguish between Whig and Jacobite clans, with the result that the loyal clans were also obliged to surrender their arms, an obligation they carried out much more diligently than their disaffected neighbours, whose ingenious efforts to conceal their stores of weapons would have defied even the most rigorous of searches. Nor could the government plead ignorance as to the true state of affairs in the Highlands. Both Duncan Forbes and Archibald, 3rd Duke of Argyll, had warned the administration of possible dangers which might arise should another Jacobite rising take place. In the autumn of 1744 Argyll had written to Henry Pelham advising him of the lack of military preparedness in the north. Pelham replied on 22 September:

> This led me to talk upon the other subject, which your Grace has so often mentioned to the king's servants, the want of arms in the hands of the friends of the government, and the little care there has been taken to disarm the enemies…What the king seems inclined to, is, that a number of spare arms should be sent down to Scotland, and delivered to such persons as your Grace shall appoint to receive them…I hope this will enable your Grace, to put your country in a better state of security, than you have hitherto thought it.

Pelham's reply shows the *ad hoc* basis on which the government's policy was based: that there were no definite guidelines established seems clear, and ministers in London appeared more adept at reacting to a crisis than anticipating one. In this case little was done to implement Pelham's proposal; indeed, when news of the rising reached Argyll, paramount chief of Clan Campbell (traditionally the most loyal of the loyal Whig clans), he refused to sanction the arming of his tenants on the grounds he had no authority to do so. This was no spurious claim. On 8 August Forbes had written:

> First the government has many more friends in the Highlands than it had in 1715, yet I do not know that there is at present any Lawful Authority that can call them forth to Action, even should occasion require it. In 1715

Archibald Campbell, 3rd Duke of Argyll (1682-1761), by Allan Ramsay. (Scottish National Portrait Gallery)

Lieutenancies were established in all the Counties. If any such thing now subsists it is more than I know.

If one of the leading lawyers in Scotland was uncertain of the legal position in 1745, then Argyll's refusal to call out and arm his men cannot be wondered at. Confusion over the correct legal procedure to be employed also created problems in England when a number of leading magnates there later tried to raise regiments in defence of the government. Moreover, the ministry needed to avoid alienating its own supporters south of the border, many of whom were deeply suspicious of moves to arm the Whig clans. Together with their Lowland Scottish brethren, the majority of Englishmen found it very difficult to differentiate between a 'loyal' Highlander and one who supported the Stuarts. In December 1745 the Earl of Chesterfield, then Viceroy of Ireland, wrote to Newcastle on this very point:

> For my own part I am very sorry to hear that any *loyall Highlanders* are to be arm'd at all. The proverb indeed says, 'set a thief to catch a thief', but I beg leave to except Scotch thieves. And I both hope and believe that those to whom I see money is given to raise loyall Highlanders will put that money in their pockets and not raise a man. Upon my word, If you give way to Scotch importunitys and jobbs upon this occasion, you will have a rebellion every seven years at least.

Geography also played a part in preventing the loyal clans from intervening during the early stages of the '45. Most of the great Whig clans — Sutherland, Mackay, Ross and Munro — inhabited the extreme north and north-east of the country, that is Sutherland, Caithness and Ross-shire. Living in these areas, remote even by Highland standards, the chiefs would have found it virtually impossible to intercept Charles on his way south, given the time it would have taken to raise their men and cross the rugged country which lay in between. That the chiefs had no weapons with which to arm the clansmen merely compounded their difficulties. The one Whig clan which was geographically well placed to frustrate Jacobite ambitions was Clan Campbell. However, in August 1745 the Campbells lacked both leadership and organisation, largely as a result of John, 2nd Duke of Argyll's misguided efforts to improve his vast estates — efforts which had weakened the position of the Campbell tacksmen who formed the bulk of the clan's officer corps. The 3rd Duke, realising that his brother's reforms had damaged the clan's military and economic structure, had begun to reverse the process. Nevertheless, at the start of the rising, this most powerful of all the Highland clans was incapable of providing a serious threat to Charles Edward, particularly in the light of Argyll's decision not to arm his men. The duke further contributed to the confusion by leaving Scotland for London where, he believed, his influence would be more usefully employed during the crisis. It was only through the efforts of Argyll's cousin, Major-General John Campbell of Mamore, that Clan Campbell eventually emerged as an effective fighting force towards the end of the rising.

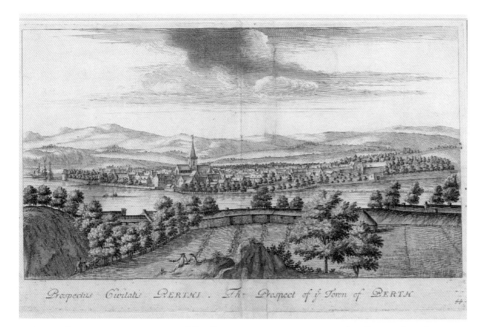

The town of Perth, from John Slezer's Theatrum Scotiae. *(National Library of Scotland)*

But these matters were of little concern to Prince Charles. After leaving Corrieyairack on 28 August the clans marched to Dalwhinnie and from there on to Dalnacardoch. On 31 August they reached Blair Castle, ancestral home of the Dukes of Atholl, where they stayed for two nights before making their way to Dunkeld. On 4 September the army reached Perth where it remained until the 10th. There had been absolutely no opposition; indeed many of the local inhabitants seemed quite delighted at the presence of the prince in their midst. On their march to Blair, Murray of Broughton reported that Charles was 'extreamly pleased with the sight of the people of the Country; men, women, and children who came running from their houses, kissing and caressing their master, who they had not seen for thirty years before, an Instance of the strongest affection, and which could not fail to move every generous mind with a mixture of grief and joy.'

Although it appeared that the gods were favouring the prince thus far, there had been a number of warning lights flickering on the way. After Cope's decision to march for Inverness became known, many of the clansmen had wished to follow him, convinced that there would be a ready supply of booty abandoned by his retreating army. Charles and his advisers correctly foresaw the difficulties which would arise if Cope's troops were pursued through the mountains by the Highlanders, who were themselves greatly fatigued by several days hard marching, and they forbade any such action. This infuriated the clansmen — whose support for their chiefs in times of conflict was at least partially motivated by the prospect of plentiful plunder at the end of a successful raid or battle — and, according to O'Sullivan, 'the Prince and the Chiefs had all the peines in the world to appaise 'um & hinder a mutenery'. Although order was restored, the dangers were there for all to see; excellent fighters though they were, the Highlanders were often unwilling to accept the conventions of eighteenth-century military discipline.

Lord George Murray (1700?-1760) was the outstanding general of the '45, but he antagonised Prince Charles almost from the start. Sir Walter Scott was to admire his stoicism in serving a master 'by whom he knew he was not beloved nor fully trusted'. Sir Compton Mackenzie considered him a defeatist: 'it was his accession to the Cause which... contributed most to its ruin'. (His Grace the Duke of Atholl's Collection at Blair Castle)

Characteristically, Charles learned nothing from the incident, with tragic consequences for both his followers and his own family.

Another cause for concern must have been the lack of recruits to the Jacobite army. At Perth the prince was joined by some 200 men under Robertson of Struan and on 11 September the Duke of Perth provided another 150 men at Dunblane. But these reinforcements were offset by a number of desertions on the march south, and by Lochiel's decision, while the Jacobites were at Dalnacardoch, to send 150 of his men home on the grounds that they were 'improperly armed'. Admittedly Charles had been joined by a number of 'gentlemen of rank' including the Duke of Perth, Lord Nairne and his brother, Mercer of Aldie, Lord Ogilvy, the Honourable William Murray of Taymount, Lord Strathallan and the Chevalier Johnstone. But while these gentlemen may have provided a much needed veneer of social respectability, the actual number of retainers who accompanied them was negligible. In fairness, some arranged for their followers and tenants to join the prince at a later date, but the lack of men recruited in an area which was widely regarded as being pro-Jacobite must have disturbed those of the prince's entourage possessing even a modicum of foresight.

On a more positive note, Lord George Murray also joined the prince at Perth. Undoubtedly the most able commander on either side during the '45, Murray's role in the rising has been the subject of much controversy. The younger brother of Tullibardine, Lord George was to figure in practically every major dispute which beset the cause over the following eight months. Much of the criticism levelled at Murray spouts from the poisoned pens of Murray of Broughton, O'Sullivan and Sir John Macdonald, all of whom

Writing to his neighbour to purchase meal twelve days after the raising of the standard at Glenfinnan, farming business may or may not have been uppermost in Lord George Murray's mind. Three weeks later, he was leading the prince's forces at the battle of Prestonpans. (National Library of Scotland, Adv.MS.82.1.3, f.247)

were either suspicious of Lord George's motives or jealous of his abilities. The mutual antipathy which existed — particularly between Murray and O'Sullivan — was ultimately to do more damage to the hopes of the Stuarts than the combined forces of Cope, Hawley and Cumberland. That this distrust prevailed from the very beginning is shown in the following extract from O'Sullivan's *Narrative*:

> My Lord George Murray joyned him there [Perth] likewise, & tho' his carracter was not of the best, & yt his own friends & relations were a feard of it, & yt some of them spook openly, especially a Lady, who told the Prince yt he cou'd not be trusted to, & yt he wou'd soon or leat ruine the Kings case; his presence nevertheless was thought necessary, to determine the Athol men to joyn, as I dont doubt but it did, tho' few or none of them had any confidence in him in the beginning.

On this occasion, fortunately, the prince chose to ignore the mutterings of his Irish clique and appointed Lord George Lieutenant-General and joint commander of the forces (under Charles) with the Duke of Perth, who shared the same rank. Charles's decision was warmly welcomed by the Highland chiefs who soon recognised Murray for what he was — a man who truly understood the Highlander and his preferred method of fighting. Lord George's Jacobite credentials were also beyond reproach: out in the '15 and the '19, Murray had fled to France following the Jacobite defeat at Glenshiel, only returning to Scotland after obtaining a royal pardon in 1725. Bitterness and acrimony lay ahead, but in early September the presence of Lord George Murray was a major boost to the morale of the clansmen as they headed south towards Edinburgh.

*****

Informed of the Jacobite army's steady advance southwards by the city's two major newspapers, the *Caledonian Mercury* and the *Edinburgh Evening Courant* (the former sympathetic to the Jacobites while the *Courant* backed the government), the citizens of Edinburgh grew increasingly restless. The southern Lowlands of Scotland was hostile territory for the Jacobites, and Edinburgh, with its population of some 50,000 (including the port of Leith) would provide the first serious military test for the prince's ramshackle army. The growing nervousness of the town's population as the Jacobites advanced was understandable. The Union of 1707 might have robbed Edinburgh of many of the trappings of a capital city, but the town was still the administrative and legal centre of Scotland, populated by judges, lawyers, senior officers of state and a whole host of middle and low-ranking civil servants ranging in importance from Commissioners of Customs and of Excise to junior clerks in the Court of Exchequer. Every person belonging to this social and political élite owed his status, livelihood and authority, directly or indirectly, to the government in London. To these people, therefore, a Jacobite victory was unthinkable — they would lose everything if James regained his crown. So, like the ungodly nervously awaiting the Second Coming, Edinburgh's ruling establishment sought to protect both themselves and their city against the advancing Highland host.

But politics and patronage would, on their own, not have provided the social cohesion necessary to enable Edinburgh and the surrounding areas to resist the Jacobite tide now apparently sweeping all before it. Presbyterianism, which was hardly compatible with the political and social philosophy of the Jacobites, dominated the southern Lowlands of Scotland. Presbyterianism had been confirmed — albeit reluctantly — by William of Orange as Scotland's state religion following the Revolution Settlement of 1689, and the Church by Law Established had a long and selective memory in which the Stuarts were forever associated with Popery and arbitrary authority. It mattered little that Charles Edward Stuart, a Roman Catholic himself, sought to reassure people of all religious persuasions by allowing them freedom of worship in those towns and communities he had occupied or passed through on his march south. As the Jacobite threat grew more serious in late August and early September, ministers seized every opportunity to remind their congregations of the dangers of flirting with Jacobitism — the hand-maiden of the anti-Christ residing at the Vatican.

This propaganda was effective, backed up as it was by the secular authorities who sought to minimise the threat posed by the Highland army while, at the same time, exaggerating the involvement of France, Spain and Rome in the rebellion. Those men who had joined the prince in his 'rash adventure', so government pamphleteers argued, were more misguided than seditious, and, by playing up France's involvement in particular, the government sought to unite the whole nation behind George II in the face of the serious external threat posed by the Catholic powers of Europe. The ruling Whigs, whose own political ideology and philosophy owed so much to the events of 1688–9, found it impossible to understand why any sane citizen of the United Kingdom should wish to return to the despotism of pre-Revolution Stuart rule. The government's attitude was reflected in contemporary newspapers and pamphlets which frequently referred to the rising north of the border as 'this unnatural rebellion'.

The outbreak of the '45 prompted a flood of 'loyal addresses' from around the country. One such address, dated 19 August, presented by the good and the great of the county of Worcester, is typical, and reflects the belief, prevalent at the time, of French complicity in the rising:

> We...being firstly filled with the highest Indignation at the daring Attempt of France to load this Free and Protestant Country with that severest Evil a Popish Pretender, as the fittest Tool for the perfidious Ambition of our most inveterate and most dangerous Enemy, who is desirous, by this Means, at once to deprive us and our Posterity of our Commerce, our Liberties and our Religion, could not satisfy our Minds after receiving such Intelligence, without embracing the first Opportunity of assuring your Majesty of our utmost Zeal and Resolution in support

of your Majesty's Government, on which, under Providence, depends the Preservation of every thing that is valuable to Englishmen and Protestants.

On 7 September the 'Lord Provost, Magistrates, and Council of the city of Edinburgh' presented their own address to the throne. After expressing the city's joy at news of George II's 'happy arrival to these your Majesty's dominions' (the king had returned to England from mainland Europe on 31 August) and vigorously condemning the current upheavals, the magistrates went on to assure their monarch of the town's loyalty by reminding him of the steadfastness shown by the citizens in 1715, when Jacobite forces briefly threatened to overrun the capital. The address concludes:

We beg leave at this time to assure your Majesty, that we will stand by you and your royal family, with our lives and fortunes; employ every power we are possess'd of, and all the means you shall put in our hands to dissapoint the views of France, and baffle the vain hopes of this rash adventurer, who has been audacious enough to attempt to darken and disturb the tranquillity of your Majesty's happy government.

It is easy to be cynical about the assurances given by the magistrates in the light of subsequent events, but the feelings and concerns expressed in the address were, at the time, undoubtedly sincere. The vast majority of Edinburgh's population — the merchants, tradesmen, shopkeepers and artisans — simply wanted to carry out their daily business without interference from politicians or kings: they most certainly did not want their lives disrupted by a major outbreak of civil disorder. The ordinary citizen plying his trade in the wynds and closes of the capital may well have been apathetic as to who wore the crown in London, but if a change of dynasty necessitated bloodshed, turmoil and tumult, then he would much rather no change took place at all. Even the *Caledonian Mercury*, which maintained a resolutely neutral position until 18 September, broke off from a report on Jacobite activity near Dundee to make the following plea for peace:

May the Lord avert a Civil War, and powerfully protect our dear native Country, which has often been signally blessed, and particularly of late with a Series of most fine Weather to reap the Fruits of the Earth.

The *Courant*, anxious to mobilise anti-Jacobite feeling and to play down the Highlanders' military prowess, adopted a different approach. The average Lowlander had a deep-rooted fear and suspicion of Highlanders, who were widely regarded as uncivilised barbarians incapable of speaking English, but perfectly capable of committing the most savage acts of atrocity. Of course these fears and prejudices were based on ignorance, an ignorance the *Courant* deliberately did nothing to dispel. In a report (also carried on 10 September) the paper described an alleged encounter between the two sides somewhere near Perth:

Edinburgh Castle. Despite the six week occupation of Edinburgh by the Jacobite army, the castle remained firmly in government hands. An attempt to blockade it was quickly called off when the garrison's commander, Lieutenant-General George Preston, ordered his artillery to fire into the town. (National Library of Scotland; on loan to the Scottish National Portrait Gallery)

The Alarm spread amongst the Highlanders, that a strong Detachment of Dragoons was abroad, and ready to attack them; on which they fled from their Camp, notwithstanding all the Remonstrances of the Chiefs, and called aloud *She pe no fight Tracoons, she pe no fight Tracoons; she pe fight Foot with her Claymore, but no Tracoons;* and with Difficulty got them persuaded to return, after it was certain it was only a false Alarm. — Not one Half of them have tolerable Arms, and as such are a pitiful ignorant crew, that such as have spread themselves to seek for Arms, are fit for nothing: They can give no Account of their Strength, of their Designs, or even of themselves; but talk of *Snishing, K. Jamesh, Reshont, Plunter, new Brogues, &c.* and diminish daily.

But Edinburgh was not to be allowed to remain undisturbed, and events leading to the town's capture often resembled high farce. Other than the two understrength regiments of dragoons and the garrisons at Stirling, Dumbarton and Edinburgh castles, Cope's departure for the north had left the Lowlands bereft of regular troops. If the city was to be defended at all then it would have to be defended by the inhabitants, and in the days following the Jacobite occupation of Perth strenuous efforts were made to strengthen the town's defences and recruit able-bodied volunteers to protect life and property. In theory, Edinburgh should have been an easy city to defend. To the south and east the town was protected by a wall built specifically for the purpose of keeping potential enemies — historically the English — at bay, while the northern approaches were blocked by a

malodorous expanse of water known (somewhat grandiloquently) as the Nor' Loch. To the west of the city stood the castle, dominating the surrounding landscape, and a symbol of invincibility throughout the ages. But appearances can be, and were, deceptive. The walls which protected the city were in an advanced state of disrepair and had been further weakened as a defensive barrier by the practice of building houses into the actual fabric of the stonework. While an attack across the Nor' Loch was unlikely — no one in their right mind would have willingly crossed that stinking morass — the castle's deterrent value was exaggerated. Although the fortress itself would have been unassailable, particularly to a Jacobite army not in possession of either field or siege artillery, the cannon on the castle ramparts could do little to prevent an attack on the city from the south or south-east, as this would involve firing into or over the town, thereby causing casualties amongst the very citizens the castle's commanders were supposed to protect. The town council had, on 7 September, issued orders for repairing and strengthening the city wall under the supervision of Colin Maclaurin, professor of mathematics at the town's college, but Maclaurin was prevented from carrying out his duties effectively because he was unable to secure the services of skilled tradesmen, who were all involved in the annual election of their deacons to the town council.

The magistrates were also hampered in their efforts to defend the capital by a serious shortage of manpower. The castle garrison was confined to the castle, and Hamilton's dragoons were not under civilian jurisdiction. There was a city guard which, in less troublesome times, was employed to maintain some semblance of order on the streets of the city — a task often beyond it due to the advanced age of many of its members and their common predilection for strong drink. That the city guard's strength was increased to 126 men as the Highlanders approached would hardly have struck terror into the hearts of Lord George Murray and his fellow commanders. In addition to the guard, the authorities were able to call upon the services of the Trained Bands — essentially a citizen's militia composed of loyal burgesses with access to the city's arsenal. These men were not, as their title suggests, trained soldiers, and their strength at the time of the rising is uncertain: the *Scots Magazine* estimated that each of the sixteen companies contained between sixty and one hundred men. As the crisis deepened, however, the magistrates sought royal approval to raise a regiment of 1000 men for the defence of the town. This approval was received on 9 September and authorised the town council to 'Raise, Form and Discipline and maintain at their own proper Charge, by voluntary Subscription of them and the other Burgesses and Inhabitants, One thousand Foot, for the Defence of the City, and Support of his Majesty's Government'. Despite initial enthusiasm, the Edinburgh Regiment (as it became known) never exceeded 250 men. It seems that the offer of sixpence a day and 'ane hatt' with a black cockade was not quite tempting enough for Edinburgh's reluctant heroes. Finally, these forces

In December 1745, Colin Maclaurin wrote to Duncan Forbes pointing out the difficulties he had had in fortifying Edinburgh: '...I laboured night & day under infinite discouragements from Superior Powers. When I was promised hundreds of Workmen I could hardly get as many dozens. This was daily complained of...but till the last two days no redress was made, and then it was [too] late...[T]here was a plain collusion.' (National Library of Scotland, MS.2969, f.46)

The Flodden Wall at Drummond Street, Edinburgh (HMSO)

A 17th century engraving of the Netherbow Port, Edinburgh. In the eighteenth century many towns and cities throughout Europe still had gates which could be closed at night. (James Grant, Cassell's Old and New Edinburgh, *1883)*

The Edinburgh city guard were only equipped to act as policeman in the town, and could not have repelled an army. (James Grant, op.cit.)

were supported by the Gentlemen Volunteers, a body of some 400 young men largely made up of students and the sons of Edinburgh's more respectable citizens. The Volunteers were divided into six companies, one of which, the College Company, was commanded by George Drummond, Commissioner of Excise and erstwhile Lord Provost of Edinburgh. Out of favour since the 1730s, Drummond hoped that the rising would provide him with a final chance to demonstrate his loyalty and attachment to the government. His resulting high profile in the defence of the city bears testimony to the dedication with which he sought to ingratiate himself with his political masters — a dedication matched only by his unrelenting pursuit of wealthy, available widows whose legacies helped to ease his own financial burdens.

On Friday 13 September Charles's army crossed the Forth at the Fords of Frew and marched to Linlithgow, arriving two days later. Gardiner's dragoons, who had boasted that they would contest any crossing of the Forth, promptly retired before the advancing Highlanders and reformed at Falkirk. There was now considerable consternation in the capital, and the daily newspaper reports which, as the Jacobites drew ever closer, became increasingly accurate and detailed, served only to heighten the alarm. At 10 a.m. on Sunday 15 September the Volunteers assembled at College Yards where Drummond gave a stirring speech informing the men that it had been decided by the officers of the crown and General Joshua Guest (senior officer in the Lowlands following Cope's departure), to engage the rebels before they reached the city. In order to ensure the success of the operation, the two regiments of dragoons had to be supported by a detachment of infantry to consist of the city guard, part of the Edinburgh Regiment and the Volunteers. Drummond's speech was answered by 'a unanimous shout of applause' which he took as an indication of the Volunteers' willingness to comply with the decision. But before the order to march was given, Drummond went round the various companies suggesting that not all the Volunteers need depart, as some would be required to man the city walls in the event of the expedition failing. This caused a considerable amount of confusion, resulting in many of the Volunteers remaining where they were, while Drummond set off for the Lawnmarket with a somewhat depleted force. On arriving at his destination Drummond must have realised what had occurred, for he then advised Lord Provost Archibald Stewart (a man many suspected of harbouring Jacobite sympathies), to ring the fire bell in order to summon reinforcements from College Yards. This had the unfortunate effect of creating panic in the town, as many of the inhabitants were attending divine service. They rushed out into the streets, uncertain as to whether the town was on fire or the Highlanders were at the gates of the city. Inadvertently, Drummond had caused, in the words of the *Scots Magazine*, 'the first appearance of fear in the place'.

In the meantime, those Volunteers who had followed Drummond to the Lawnmarket awaited further orders. Alexander Carlyle, one of the Volunteers in the College Company, recalled what happened next:

During this halt [at the Lawnmarket], Hamilton's Dragoons, who had been at Leith, marched past our Corps, on their route to join Gardiner's regiment who were at the Colt Bridge. We cheered them, in passing, with a huzzah, and the spectators began to think at last that some serious fighting was likely to ensue, though before this moment many of them laughed and ridiculed the volunteers. While we remained there, which was the greatest part of an hour, the mobs in the street and the ladies in the windows treated us very variously, many with lamentation, and even with tears, and some apparent scorn and derision.

After being reinforced by some companies which responded to the call of the fire bell, the Volunteers marched down the West Bow towards the Grassmarket and West Port from where they would leave the security of the city. On the way, however, many were 'persuaded' by friends and relatives to abandon the enterprise. Few required much persuading: this was clearly no longer an exercise, and the very real prospect of being killed or maimed resulted in the rapid dispersal of the gallant band. David Hume later likened the march of the Volunteers from the Lawnmarket to the West Port 'to the course of the Rhine, which rolling pompously its Waves through the fertile fields…is continually drawn off by a thousand canals, and, at last, becomes a small rivulet, which loses itself in the sand before it reaches the ocean'.

By the time they reached the Grassmarket only some forty men remained, and even they were subject to the exhortations of the clergy who were

The city guardhouse, opposite where the Edinburgh City Chambers now stand. (James Grant, op.cit.)

Bonnie Prince Charlie's Cottage, Duddingston. A 19th century view. (James Grant, op.cit.)

PLAN OF ARTHUR'S SEAT (THE SANCTUARY OF HOLYROOD).

A plan of Arthur's Seat. (James Grant, op.cit.)

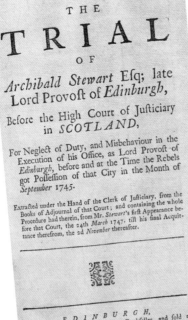

THE
TRIAL
OF

Archibald Stewart Efq; late
Lord Provoft of *Edinburgh*,

Before the High Court of Jufticiary
in *SCOTLAND*,

For Neglect of Duty, and Misbehaviour in the
Execution of his Office, as Lord Provoft of
Edinburgh, before and at the Time the Rebels
got Poffeffion of that City in the Month of
September 1745.

Extracted under the Hand of the Clerk of Jufticiary, from the
Books of Adjournal of that Court; and containing the whole
Procedure had therein, from Mr. *Stewart's* firft Appearance before that Court, the 24th *March* 1747. till his final Acquit-
tance therefrom, the 2d *November* thereafter.

E D I N B U R G H,
Printed for GIDEON CRAWFURD Bookfeller, and fold at
his Shop in the *Parliament-Clofe*: and by the other Bookfel-
lers in Town and Country. 1747.

After being acquitted at his trial in Edinburgh, Archibald Stewart, the former Lord Provost of the town, was taken to London to be tried, but acquitted there also. (National Library of Scotland, Nha.V125 (5))

anxious to avoid unnecessary bloodshed. At 2.30 p.m., Drummond, who had earlier disappeared, returned and marched the remnants back to College Yards. The next day, the Volunteers disbanded and returned their arms to the castle, and Drummond's hopelessly ineffectual attempts at defending the city were finally at an end. Although Carlyle refuted the allegations, he felt obliged to record that 'some of the Volunteers imagined that this manoeuvre about the Volunteers was entirely Drummond's, and that he had no mind to face the rebels, though he had made a parade of courage and zeal to make himself popular'. Despite Carlyle's defence of the former provost, there can be little doubt that Drummond fully intended his actions to be noticed by those in authority. He was not disappointed in these hopes: in recognition of his 'services', he was rewarded with the provost's ermine on a further five occasions between 1746 and his death twenty years later.

The senior officers of the crown departed the city on Monday morning, leaving Provost Stewart in an impossible position. As confusion and uncertainty spread, news reached Edinburgh that the Highlanders had passed through Winchburgh and Kirkliston and were now heading for Corstorphine, two miles west of the city. Stewart was faced with two stark choices: he could defend the city with his meagre forces, or he could surrender it to Charles Edward Stuart. Either way he was probably damned. If he resisted and failed, the Jacobites might wreak a terrible vengeance on the town and its inhabitants; if he surrendered and Cope then arrived at Leith in the transports which had sailed from Aberdeen on the 15th and defeated the rebels, he might well be accused of treason and punished accordingly. (Stewart did stand trial after the rising, charged with 'neglect of duty', but the court eventually, and sensibly, found him not guilty.) Throughout the day the beleaguered provost held meetings with his fellow magistrates and other leading citizens. Both General Guest — secure in the castle — and the officers of state — safely out of harm's way — offered to provide military assistance in the form of the dragoons should he, Stewart, so request. Unable to decide, and unwilling to act without specific written instructions, the provost's mind was made up for him by the sight of both regiments of dragoons fleeing along the Lang Dykes (site of present day Princes Street) towards Leith. This heroic body of horsemen had been fired upon by an advance party of the Highland army at Colt Bridge, and was now retreating in some disorder and at considerable speed. Deprived of the support of regular troops, distraught citizens now pleaded with Stewart to surrender the city rather than risk widespread slaughter.

In the midst of this mayhem a letter was presented to the provost and read aloud to the crowd assembled in the New Church. The letter began, 'Whereas we are now ready to enter the beloved Metropolis of our Ancient Kingdom of Scotland…' Upon hearing this, George Drummond asked who the signatory was, and, on being informed it was none other than 'Charles, Prince Regent of the Kingdoms of Scotland, England, France and Ireland', immediately ordered the reading to cease. This resulted in further uproar, and the provost and magistrates retired to the relative peace of Goldsmith's Hall. By now Charles had reached Slateford, on the outskirts of the city, and set up his headquarters at Gray's Mill; his letter to the magistrates amounted to little more than an ultimatum. Calling on the authorities to surrender the city and the arms and ammunition therein, the communication concluded, 'if any opposition be made to us, we cannot answer for the consequences, being firmly resolved to enter the city; and in that case, if any of the inhabitants are found in arms against us, they must not be expected to be treated as prisoners of war'.

The chilling tone of the letter removed any lingering doubts the magistrates might have entertained; the city would have to surrender. It was agreed, however, that a deputation should be sent to the prince, pleading for more time to consider the matter. Ironically, shortly after the deputation left the city, news came in that Cope's fleet of transports had been sighted in the Forth. Baillie James Mansfield, a man renowned for his Jacobitism, was sent to call the deputation back, but he returned shortly afterwards to report the 'failure' of his mission.

On their arrival at Charles's headquarters, Murray of Broughton was delegated to meet with the deputies, who told him that the town council desired the prince to let them know what was expected of them. Murray replied that his master 'required no further than that they should open their gates to his army and delivre up the arms of the Town and garrison, with the ammunition and Military Stores then in the Town, in which case the liberties of the City should be preserved, and all necessary protection given them'. On hearing this, the deputation then asked to be given time to discuss these terms with the whole council, and the prince ordered Murray to allow the city 'two or three hours to bring back an answer, but grant them no further respite, having good intelligence that they desired no more than to dallie of the time till they saw how far it was possible for them to be relieved by Gl. Cope'.

It is clear from Murray's account that Charles was in no mood to be dictated to by the magistrates of Edinburgh. Anticipating further attempts at delay, the prince ordered Lochiel to 'putt his people under arms' in case there was a need to effect a military solution should negotiations fail. This detachment, perhaps 900 strong, was to be commanded by Lochiel and O'Sullivan, with Murray of Broughton acting as guide. Charles's suspicions were well founded. The deputation did not return to Edinburgh until 10 p.m. where, after much discussion, a further embassy was sent to Gray's Mill asking for an additional seven hours grace. This request was summarily dismissed and the second deputation returned to Edinburgh at about 3 a.m. Murray takes up the story:

The detachment had immediately orders to march…taking the road by Merkistown and Hopes Park, where they passed without being observed by the garrison in the Castle, tho so near as to hear them distinctly call

George Drummond (1687-1766). Drummond rebuilt his faltering political career on the strength of the loyalty he displayed to the government during the '45. He went on to play a prominent part in the planning of Edinburgh's celebrated New Town. (National Library of Scotland; on loan to the Scottish National Portrait Gallery)

their rounds, and arrived at the nether bow Port without meeting any body on their way, and found the wall of the Town which flanks the Pleasants and St. Marys wind mounted with cannon, but no person appeared. Locheil ordered one of his people in a great coat and hunting cape to go and demand entrance att the gate, while he was ready to have followed him in case he had obtained admittance, but the fellow being refused access, and it now being clear daylight, Mr M[urray] proposed to retire to a place call'd St Leonards hills, and after securing themselves from the cannon of the Castle, to waite for orders from the Chevalier where to attack the town, that tho they had it then in their power to force their entry by any of the houses in st Marys wind which makes part of the Town wall, yett their orders of moderation were so severe that they could not take it upon them to demolish any of the houses without liberty given. This retreat being thus agreed to Mr M. went to the rear of the detachment to make them march and guide them to the place proposed, but before he had time to get so far, the Coach which had returned with the deputies came down the High Street and oblidged the Guard to open the Port, upon which Locheil took the advantage and rushed in, the guard immediately dispersing. Thus did the Chevalier render himself master of the Capital without shedding a drop of Blood.

While Edinburgh got ready to receive Prince Charles, a few miles down the coast the town of Dunbar awaited the arrival of General Cope.

4 PRESTONPANS

They [the Highlanders] received a very full fire from Right to Left of the Enemy, which killed severals; but advancing up, they discharged and threw down their Muskets, and drawing their broad Swords, gave a most frightful and hideous Shout, rushing most furiously upon the Enemy, so that in 7 or 8 minutes, both Horse and Foot were totally routed and drove from the Field of Battle; though it must be owned that the Enemy fought very gallantly, but they could not withstand the Impetuosity, or rather Fury of the Highlanders, and were forced to run when they could no longer resist.

(THE CALEDONIAN MERCURY, 23 SEPTEMBER 1745)

Oh England what will become of thy Laws, Religion and Liberty, when such madness is gone out; Merciful God send us help from Heaven and honest courageous soldiers to fight our battles.

(LADY HARDWICKE TO HER SON THE HON. PHILIP YORKE, 28 SEPTEMBER 1745)

ON the morning of 18 September, with the town now safely secured, Charles Edward Stuart was free to make his triumphal entry into Scotland's capital city. After arriving at the King's Park by a somewhat circuitous route (in order to avoid being fired upon by the guns on the castle ramparts), the prince made his way towards Holyrood Palace. Flanked by the Jacobite nobility and the clan chiefs, Charles made slow progress due to the huge crowd which had gathered to witness his arrival — a crowd whose presence was motivated more by curiosity than by loyalty to his family. The *Caledonian Mercury*, which now gleefully abandoned its previous impartiality, reported that the prince 'was met by 20000 of the Citizens of Edinburgh, huzzaing and welcoming his Highness. The Crowd

Poems written by ladies, in praise of Prince Charles. (National Library of Scotland, MS.2960, f.79; RB.l.70)

Andrew Fletcher, Lord Milton to Sir John Cope:

'Edinburgh 5 Septr 1745

'Sir, According to your desire General Guest has
showed the Advocate the Sollicitor and me your
Letter to him dated at Inverness the 31 Aug:
last requiring our assistance in providing
Transports for the Troops under your
Command to be sent to you from Leith to
Inverness. And the making answer has been
put upon me.

'As you must know much better than we (can
guess at) your difficultys of bringing South
his Majesty's Forces under your Command
any other way than by Sea, no time has been
lost to put it [sic] your power to take that
Route, Captain Beavour of the Fox Man of war is
here and undertaking to go Convoy, and those employed to agree with the
Transports make no doubt of getting the 2000 tun you mention at Leith.

'But if the information we have reason to rely on be just, That the great Body of
the Highland Insurgents are at Perth, whither your passage with the Forces under
your Command by Land would not be very practicable must be submitted to your
Superiour knowledge in these Matters, and there is this great difference betwixt the
Two Methods, that if the Forces are Embarked it depends on the Winds, how Soon
they can arrive and Land in the South, possibly it may be weeks, and time in this
conjuncture seems precious. I am with great Regards.
Sir

'Your most obedient and most humble Servant
And Fletcher

'Yesternight the Stores and Gunners from London arrived at Leith & proceeded yt
day to the Castle. It was thought proper to send you this by a ferry boat Express.'

(*National Library of Scotland, MS.2960, ff.86b r.&v.*)

was so throng, that he that got an Opportunity of kissing his Boot, thought
himself very happy. Greater Demonstrations of Joy was never seen since the
Restoration of King Charles II.'

Even allowing for the *Mercury's* hyperbole, there can be little doubt that
the pageantry and splendour of the occasion made a vivid impression on
those who were present that day. This sense of occasion was further
heightened by the ceremony which took place at the city's Mercat Cross
where the town's heralds and pursuivants proclaimed James King of

Scotland, England, France and Ireland, and read out the Commission of Regency and the prince's own declaration to the assembled onlookers. That this ceremony was taking place in Edinburgh at all must have filled the watching Whigs with despair; a few weeks earlier such an occurrence would have been inconceivable, even to the most fanatical of Jacobites. Yet the reality was that within a month of raising his father's standard at Glenfinnan, Charles had made himself master of Scotland's capital. The one consolation for government supporters was that Cope's army had landed at Dunbar and would surely now march to relieve the city.

It took Cope the best part of two days to disembark at Dunbar before setting out for Haddington, where he arrived on the 19th. The following morning, the army continued its march towards Edinburgh, turning northwards towards the village of Tranent. On receiving reports that the Jacobites were at Musselburgh, Cope positioned his forces north of Tranent on a flat plain ideally suited for both his infantry and cavalry. He had also taken care to provide adequate cover for his troops: to the south was an expanse of marshy ground punctuated by hedges, dry-stane dykes and a series of open ditches used for draining the swamp, while to the west the General's right flank was protected by the ten-foot high walls surrounding Preston House and by the enclosures of Bankton House, the home of Colonel Gardiner. Finally, the rear of the position was guarded by the sea and the villages of Port Seton, Cockenzie and Prestonpans. Here, in ground of his own choosing, Cope awaited the arrival of the enemy he had avoided at Corrieyairack.

The response was not long in coming. Reaching Musselburgh, Lord George was informed that the enemy was in the vicinity of Preston and, displaying a sound knowledge of local topography, he determined to gain the high ground south of Cope's position. By early afternoon the Highlanders had reached their objective, the crest of Falside Hill, but the sight of Cope's army in a strong defensive position below them had a disheartening effect on the Jacobite commanders. Already there had been signs of disharmony in the ranks over who should have the honour of forming the right wing of the army in the event of a battle taking place — an honour the Macdonalds believed was theirs by right — and it was only through the prompt intervention of Lochiel and Murray himself that a major crisis was avoided. Now, when co-operation was most required in deciding upon a suitable plan of attack, communication between the various commanders almost broke down completely. Charles, anxious to prevent Cope from abandoning his position and marching off to recapture Edinburgh, ordered the Atholl Brigade to take up position on the Musselburgh road to block any such attempt. Lord George was furious when he learned of this, and in a fit of temper threw his gun on the ground and 'swore God he'd never draw his sword for the cause if the Brigade was not brought back'. Faced with the prospect of alienating his lieutenant-general on the eve of battle, Charles complied with Murray's demands, much to the disgust of O'Sullivan and Sir John Macdonald, who regarded Murray's behaviour towards the prince as

Holyrood Palace, Edinburgh. Prince Charles was the first royal visitor to entertain guests in the palace since the brief reign of his grandfather, James II, in the 1680s. However, the palace being exposed to the castle's guns made it prudent for the prince to lodge in a cottage at Duddingston, on the other side of Arthur's Seat. (National Library of Scotland; on loan to the Scottish National Portrait Gallery)

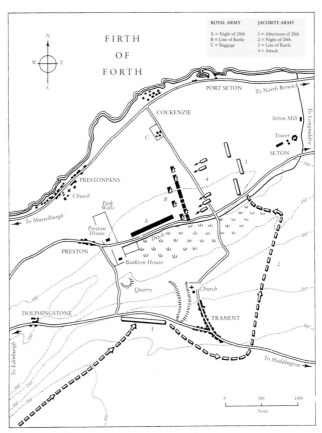

The battle of Prestonpans, 21 September 1745.

being totally unacceptable. Matters were hardly improved by Lord George's decision — taken without consulting his fellow officers — to attack Cope from the east, resulting in Clan Cameron having to march across the front of Cope's army in order to take up their new station for the proposed assault. Concerned that all this movement in the Jacobite ranks signalled the beginning of an attack by both flanks of the Highland army, Cope ordered his own forces to take up new positions facing the south-west and slightly to the west of his original deployment.

Murray's plan to attack the unprotected left flank of Cope's army by marching around the eastern end of the marsh was adopted by his fellow officers during that evening's council of war. The attack was planned for first light the following morning, and all those who attended the meeting must have been acutely aware that the future of the rising depended on the outcome of the forthcoming battle. Both armies were remarkably even in terms of manpower, each side numbering between 2000 and 2500 men, the prince having been reinforced by 250 men commanded by Lord Nairne and 150 clansmen under Maclachlan of Maclachlan before he left Edinburgh. The advantages which Cope appeared to hold over his Jacobite opponents, namely Hamilton's and Gardiner's two regiments of dragoons and a number of light field pieces and mortars, were more than offset by a complete lack of trained artillerymen and the poor state of the dragoons' morale, which had been shattered during their panic-driven retreat a few days previously. However, despite the Jacobites' seizure of over 1000 stand of arms belonging to the city guard and the Trained Bands, Cope's infantry were still better equipped than their Highland opponents, some of whom resorted to carrying scythes mounted on poles in the absence of anything more suitable. It remained to be seen whether the better equipped, but poorly trained and untested Hanoverian infantry would be capable of withstanding the fearsome impact of a Highland charge.

The fortunes of the Jacobites were given an unexpected boost that night. Robert Anderson of Whitburgh, son of a local laird, informed the Jacobite commanders of a narrow track which ran through the marsh to the front of Cope's position. If the prince's army were to take this route rather than marching all the way around the marsh, it would save a considerable amount of time, and bring them closer to the flank of the enemy. Anderson's suggestion was immediately adopted by Murray and, shortly before 4 a.m., the Jacobites began their march through the bog. The army, moving silently in the darkness, was led by the Macdonalds (who were to take the right) followed by Perth's men and the Macgregors, while the Stewarts of Appin

The flamboyant Lord Mark Kerr was rumoured to have greeted Sir John Cope at the gates of Berwick with the remark that he was the first general in history to bring news of his own defeat. Cope was later exonerated by a board of enquiry, and is said to have won a fortune by wagering that the next general sent to meet the rebels would suffer the same fate. (National Library of Scotland; on loan to the Scottish National Portrait Gallery)

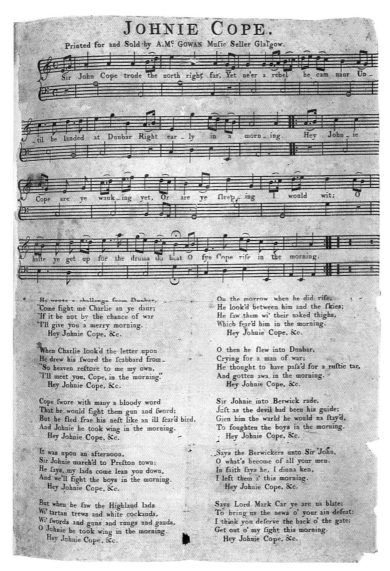

One of the best known Scottish songs, 'Johnie Cope' was written by a local man soon after the battle of Prestonpans, and published to great acclaim. (National Library of Scotland, MS.2960, f.86)

and the Camerons brought up the rear. Behind these front-line troops came the reserve, consisting of the Atholl Brigade and the newly arrived Maclachlans. The Duke of Perth commanded the right of the army, the left was under Murray, and the prince and Lord Nairne led the reserve. On reaching the plain, about 1000 yards east of Cope's left flank, the Highland front line began to take up its position for the attack, but, before the reserve was clear of the marsh, Cope's scouts detected the movements of the Highlanders and a gun was fired to raise the alarm. Responding rapidly, Cope's army turned through ninety degrees and faced the approaching Jacobites, their right flank protected by the morass while the left pointed towards the village of Cockenzie. The infantry were posted in the centre with two squadrons of Hamilton's dragoons on the left, Gardiner's on the right, and a further two squadrons in the reserve. All Cope's artillery was placed on the right of his army, drastically reducing its effectiveness.

Prestonpans, or Gladsmuir as it was known to the Jacobites, was not so much a battle as a rout. From beginning to end the whole affair could not have lasted more than fifteen minutes and, while accounts differ in detail, most observers agree that Cope's army — both infantry and cavalry — broke immediately the Highlanders smashed into their lines. The following account of what Robert Wightman, former treasurer of Edinburgh town council, later called 'the scuffle of Prestonpans' comes from the same officer who was with Cope at Corrieyairack:

> Three large bodies in columns of their pick'd out Highlanders, came in a-pace, though in a collected body, with great swiftness. And the column which was advancing towards our right, where our train was posted, after receiving the discharge of a few pieces, almost in an instant, and before day broke, seiz'd the train, and threw into the utmost confusion a body of about 100 foot of ours, who was posted there to guard it. All remedies, in every shape, were tried by the general, brigadier *Fowke*, the earls of *Loudon* and *Hume*, and the officers about them, to remedy this disorder, but in vain. This, unhappily, with the fire made (tho' a very irregular one) by the Highland column on our right, struck such a panick into our dragoons, that in a moment they fled, and left *Gardner*, their colonel, (who was heard to call upon them to stand) to receive the wounds which left him on the field. His lieutenant colonel, *Whitney*, while within his horses length of him, coming up with his squadron to attack them, received a shot which shatter'd his arm, and was left by his squadron too. And from this example, the whole body became possess'd with the same fatal dread, so that it became utterly impossible for the general, or any one of the best intentioned of his officers, either to put an end to their fears, or stop their flight.

Having successfully rallied about 450 of the dragoons, Cope, together with a number of his senior officers, managed to make his way to Berwick and safety. With the exception of some 200 infantry who also managed to escape, the rest of Cope's army were either dead, wounded or captured.

Cairn at Prestonpans marking the site of the battle on 21 September 1745. In the middle ages it had been prophesied that the Scots would win a great victory against the English at Gladsmuir. Many Highlanders believed the prophecy had come true, as the hamlet of that name was only a few miles away. Soon afterwards, the inhabitants of Prestonpans laid claim to the battle, hoping to benefit from an influx of sightseers. (HMSO)

Jacobite casualties were minimal, between twenty and thirty men having been killed and some fifty wounded. Most of the government losses occurred as the retreating soldiers tried to clamber through breaches made in the walls surrounding Preston House: there the broadsword-wielding clansmen inflicted horrendous injuries on the panic-stricken mass as they desperately tried to evade their pursuers. It took a considerable effort on the part of Lord George and other Highland officers to limit the scale of the slaughter, but they were unable to stop the clansmen from plundering and stripping the bodies of the dead and wounded, an enterprise in which they were willingly and ably assisted by a number of local inhabitants. Almost 1500 prisoners were taken by the Highlanders; of the officers who were later released on parole, most subsequently broke their promise not to take up arms against the prince 'while the affair lasted', presumably on the grounds that any such undertaking given to rebels in arms was not morally binding.

The prince returned to Edinburgh the following day and expressly prohibited any public celebrations to mark his victory — a victory which had resulted in the death of a number of his father's subjects. But if there were to be no public demonstrations of joy, no one in the Jacobite camp could have failed to appreciate the magnitude of the prince's achievements. Apart from the garrisons remaining in Lowland castles and Highland forts, Scotland was now free of Hanoverian troops; Charles had, temporarily at least, regained one of his father's kingdoms. But this euphoria also brought danger: after Prestonpans the prince became convinced that the blue-bonneted Highlander with his plaid, targe, dirk and broadsword, was a far superior fighter than his Hanoverian counterpart. This ignored a number of crucial factors. The morale of the government troops at Prestonpans was poor and they lacked effective leadership. Cope's men were not the seasoned

An enlistment notice issued by the Jacobite army, 26 September 1745. (National Library of Scotland, MS.2960, f.80)

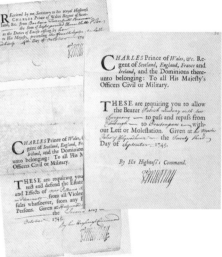

A receipt and safe conducts issued at Edinburgh by Prince Charles's secretary, John Murray of Broughton. (National Library of Scotland, MS.2960, f.78; Adv.MS.23.3.26, f.30 & f.31r.&v.)

James Rattray's commission as major in the Duke of Atholl's regiment, signed by Prince Charles. (National Library of Scotland, MS.940, f.7)

Sir Robert Strange's engraving of Prince Charles, the only one known to have been made during the '45. (National Library of Scotland; on loan to the Scottish National Portrait Gallery)

veterans of Dettingen or Fontenoy whose experiences on the battlefields of Flanders would make them unlikely to run off at the first sight of a screaming horde of semi-naked Highlanders brandishing broadswords. Moreover, the prince's army had not yet faced a sustained, accurate artillery bombardment, nor had they received concentrated volleys of musket fire at close range from infantry trained to fire two or three rounds a minute to devastating effect. The Highlanders did everything asked of them at Prestonpans, and Charles was right to praise their efforts; but, with his customary reluctance to accept unpalatable truths, the prince managed to confuse bravery with invincibility.

Victory also presented Charles with a major dilemma: should he follow up the rout of Cope's army by pursuing the remnants to Berwick, or should he remain at Edinburgh to consolidate his position? Some of his followers (and some of his opponents) believed that had he marched south immediately and taken advantage of the considerable disarray which prevailed in Hanoverian circles, then London would have been his for the taking. But this was simply not a practical proposition in the days following Prestonpans. The prince's army was far too small for such an enterprise. Some of the clansmen, suitably burdened with plunder, had already gone home after Prestonpans, and more were needed to guard the prisoners. Murray of Broughton estimated that Charles could depend on no more than 1500 men to follow him at this stage, and it was highly likely that some of these would desert as they neared the English border. Reinforcements were desperately needed, and Broughton believed that Edinburgh was the 'only proper place to waite for a junction, find provisions, provid things necessary for his army, find recruits, horses &c., and raise the publick money'. Charles was persuaded, and his army remained in Edinburgh for a further six weeks.

The next major difficulty the prince had to contend with was the castle and its garrison. Determined to prevent supplies from reaching the beleaguered force, Charles stationed troops at the head of the Lawnmarket.

Extracts from the Caledonian Mercury *reporting events following the battle of Prestonpans. (National Library of Scotland)*

John Campbell 'of the Bank' (d.1771), by William Mosman. A second cousin of the Duke of Argyll, John Campbell was appointed Cashier of the Royal Bank of Scotland in 1745, and dealt with the Jacobites in person while their army was in Edinburgh. When this portait was painted, in 1749, it was technically illegal for a Highland gentleman to dress in the manner depicted — the authorities, however, had no doubts about Campbell's loyalty. (Courtesy of the Royal Bank of Scotland plc)

General Preston, who commanded the castle garrison, demanded that the blockade be lifted, and threatened to fire on the town if his demands were not met. Charles refused, and Preston kept his word. For several days the cannonade continued; a number of people were killed and property on Castlehill was severely damaged or set on fire. The citizens pleaded with the prince to call off the siege, and on 5 October Charles agreed, anxious not to further alienate the local inhabitants. The prince deserves credit for his decision: he undoubtedly lost face over the affair, but was prepared to abandon his strategic objectives in response to public opinion. His opponents were never to be so generous.

Money, or rather lack of it, remained a pressing problem. The 4000 *louis d'or* brought from France had been used up by the time Charles reached Perth, and there was now an urgent need to replenish Jacobite coffers. Cope's war chest, containing some £3000, had been seized after Prestonpans, but more hard cash was required. The Royal Bank of Scotland, together with its rival the Bank of Scotland, had removed all specie to the castle before Charles reached Edinburgh, but later agreed to honour notes to the value of over

David Wemyss, Lord Elcho (1721-1787), probably by Domenico Dupra. The eldest son of the 4th Earl of Wemyss, Lord Elcho visited the Stuarts at Rome in 1740 and served in the prince's Lifeguards in the '45, as well as making Prince Charles a loan of 1500 guineas in September 1745. When the money was not subsequently repaid, relations between them soured, and Elcho became one of the prince's most bitter critics. (In the collection of the Earl of Wemyss)

£3500 presented by Murray of Broughton. Letters were also sent to all the burghs in Scotland, to collectors of the cess (land tax), to collectors and comptrollers of the Customs and Excise and to the factors on the forfeited estates, ordering them 'to produce their books, and to pay the balances due to them...on pain of being deemed, and treated as rebels'. The *Scots Magazine*, which remained admirably impartial throughout the rising, reported that, 'great numbers found themselves forced to comply'. A deputation was also sent to Glasgow to enforce an earlier demand for £15,000, but the canny burgesses of that Whig town negotiated a compromise whereby the prince only received £5000 in cash and £500 worth of goods.

While some progress was being made on the financial front, the number of recruits to the prince's army remained disappointingly small. Certainly a number of Lowland lords and gentlemen joined Charles at Edinburgh, among them the Honourable Arthur Elphinstone (later Lord Balmerino), the Earl of Kilmarnock and Lord Pitsligo, but none of the great southern magnates would have anything to do with the prince. Tullibardine, Glenbucket, Lord Lewis Gordon and Lord Ogilvy made strenuous efforts to provide more men (mainly from the north-east Lowlands), and the existing clan regiments were augmented. Mackinnon of Mackinnon and his clan, together with 100 Macgregors of Balquidder, also arrived. Just as Charles was leaving Edinburgh, Cluny Macpherson came up with over 300 of his men, providing a welcome last minute addition to the prince's army. A cavalry arm and a small artillery train were also raised, the latter furnished by guns captured at Prestonpans. But despite the efforts of Charles's adherents and the victory over Cope, there was no snowball effect resulting in vast numbers flocking to the Stuart standard. Lovat (who did not send his clan out until December), and others, still prevaricated, and it was clear that the great Skye chieftains were now irrevocably lost to the cause. Consequently, the Jacobite army that finally left Edinburgh consisted of no more than 5000 foot and 500 cavalry, probably less than half the forces available to Wade at Newcastle.

It was while the prince remained at Edinburgh that the first signs of serious divisions within the Jacobite high command became apparent. In order to facilitate and co-ordinate policy and administration, Charles formed a council which met every morning in his drawing room at Holyrood Palace. Initially consisting of seventeen members (excluding Charles), the council gradually split into two distinct factions: one group backed the prince, the other followed Lord George Murray. Lord Elcho believed that this split was the result of the prince's arbitrary and authoritarian behaviour at council meetings, where he was usually supported by O'Sullivan, Sheridan, Broughton, Perth, Nairne and Pitsligo, who accepted the basic premise that 'Kings and Princes Can never act or think wrong'. The other members (Murray, Gordon, Elcho, Ogilvy, Lochiel, Keppoch, young Clanranald, Ardshiel, Glencoe, Lochgarry and Glenbucket), who formed a clear majority on the council, believed that no man was infallible, and complained that the prince 'Could not bear to hear any body differ in Sentiment from him, and took a dislike to Every body that did, for he had a Notion of Commanding the army As any General does a body of Mercenaries, and so lett them know only what he pleased, and they obey without inquiring further about the matter.'

It was not only the prince's personality which created divisions: the strategy to be employed now that the army had increased in strength also needed to be agreed. Charles Edward was never in any doubt that securing Scotland was merely the first stage on the road to recovering *all* his father's kingdoms. He believed that an invasion of England was the next logical move, and was so convinced of this himself that he never seriously contemplated any opposition from his commanders. But at the council of war held on 30 October, Lord George and the chiefs made it clear that they would not simply rubber-stamp any proposal to invade England. The Highlanders favoured further consolidation in Scotland; more men needed to be recruited before they could risk engaging the vastly superior forces now assembling south of the border. Indeed, some of those present believed that they had already fulfilled their obligation to the prince; they had rallied to his cause in order to restore the Stuarts to the throne of Scotland — no one had mentioned that they might be required to do the same for England. If Wade came north then they would willingly fight again for their prince, but only on Scottish soil.

A page from the Caledonian Mercury, *Friday 11 October 1745. (National Library of Scotland)*

Against this the prince had a number of persuasive arguments of his own. To begin with, all those present realised the danger posed by prolonged inactivity. If the army stayed where it was then the Highlanders would slowly but surely slip away, back to their native hills. These men quickly grew bored with endless reviews and drilling; they needed action. There was also the danger, as Broughton pointed out, that remaining in Edinburgh would soften them, and the Highlanders, 'little accustomed to the effeminacy to[o] common in town, might be debauched both by women and drink, which would render them less able for the fatigue they must of necessity go through'. Charles also argued that a Scottish invasion of England would not only encourage the English Jacobites to rise, but also persuade the French to intervene decisively on their behalf.

Charles had been able to play the French card more effectively ever since the arrival on 14 October of Alexandre de Boyer, Marquis d'Eguilles. D'Eguilles had been sent by Louis XV to ascertain the effectiveness of the prince's army, assess the strength of pro-Jacobite sentiment in Britain and discover Charles's future intentions. The Frenchman's true role was never made public, but the very presence of an emissary from the King of France made Charles's claim that the French would support his cause appear far more plausible. Taken in conjunction with the arrival of four French ships laden with stores and artillery at Stonehaven and Montrose, it did indeed seem as if the French were finally rousing themselves. To remain inactive in Scotland, argued Charles, would serve only to delay French intervention, and

Num. 3901

The Caledonian Mercury.

Edinburgh, Monday, October 14, 1745.

Declaration by Prince Charles, printed in the Caledonian Mercury, *14 October 1745. At one point, he breezily sums up events to date: 'I, with my own Money, hire a small Vessel, ill provided with Money, Arms or Friends; I arrive in Scotland, attended by seven Persons; I publish the King my Father's Declaration, and proclaim his Title with Pardon in one Hand, and in the other Liberty of Conscience, and the most solemn Promises to grant whatever a free Parliament shall propose for the Happiness of a People...'* (National Library of Scotland)

would enable the British government to increase its forces to the point where they would inevitably overwhelm the Jacobite army. But the argument that the English would rise in support once the Highlanders crossed the border found little support in council. The English Jacobites, according to the Scots, were not to be trusted, their commitment to the House of Stuart being limited to 'Womanish Railing, vain Boasting, and noisy Gasconades'.

In the end the prince's arguments proved the more persuasive, although he carried the day by only one vote. Charles also insisted that Wade, then believed to be at Newcastle, should be attacked immediately. This was a high-risk strategy: if the Jacobites were defeated then the rising would be over; there would be little opportunity to retreat and regroup while in hostile territory. In fact the prince realised that time was against him; if Wade was defeated quickly and decisively, then not only would the French have no further reason for delay, but the English Jacobites and the reluctant Highland clans would undoubtedly come over to his side. But Lord George rejected this course of action and proposed, as Elcho describes, an alternative strategy:

Lord George, to bring a medium betwixt all these reasonings, proposed to the Prince Since he would Go to England to go to Cumberland, where, he

Said, he knew the Country, That the Army would be well Situated to receive reinforcements from Scotland to join the French when they Landed, or the English if they rose, and that it was a Good Country to fight Wades Army in, because of the Mountanious Ground in it which is the fittest for the Highlanders, and then his (Wades) Army would be fatigued after a winters march across a bad country.

The following morning the prince reluctantly agreed to Murray's plan, and the army packed up for its fateful march south, leaving the Viscount of Strathallan to raise another Jacobite army north of the Forth.

*****

English reaction to Prestonpans was one of shocked disbelief. Those ministers who believed that the rising was merely a local affair, destined to collapse at the first appearance of Cope's army, were quickly jolted out of their complacency. On 2 October Andrew Mitchell, under secretary to Tweeddale, wrote to Duncan Forbes from Whitehall that Cope's defeat had 'justly occasioned a very great alarm here', resulting in 'a run upon the Bank, which is now happily stopped, by the numerous Association of the principal Merchants to receive & make payments in Bank Notes'. But bankers and

Throughout the rebellion there was a steady output of propaganda aimed at stiffening resolve on the government side. Some of it amounted to little more than wishful thinking. (National Library of Scotland; on loan to the Scottish National Portrait Gallery)

financiers were not the only group to feel threatened by the news from Scotland. Judging by the correspondence of the time there were many others who believed that the whole structure of British society was in imminent danger of collapsing, as the following letter from the Lord Chancellor's son, Charles Yorke, to his brother Joseph clearly illustrates:

> It is indeed a dreadful and amazing consideration to reflect that the work of so many wise and honest men, of so many parliaments of fifty seven years, that a fabric of so much art and cost as the Revolution and its train of consequences, should be in danger of being overwhelmed by the bursting of a cloud, which seemed, at first gathering, no bigger than a man's hand. If France and Spain should be invited, as unquestionably they are, by this rapid progress, to make some descent on England, in order to carry on the scheme which they have laid for our ruin, who knows what blood may be shed in the quarrel, what turns it may give to matters on the Continent? The Pretender himself, being successful, would come in [not only?] as a slave to those courts, but as a conqueror over us without terms of limitation and hungry priests and courtiers would eat up the fat of the land.

It was this fear of France — so eloquently expressed in Yorke's letter — which intensified English anxiety in the weeks following Prestonpans. The government remained convinced that France had encouraged Charles Edward in his enterprise; it was inconceivable to ministers that the prince might have acted independently, and they assumed that it would only be a matter of time before Louis XV provided him with more tangible support. On the very day Cope's army was destroyed by the Jacobites, Newcastle had confessed to the Duke of Richmond, 'I am very apprehensive, that the Pretender's son being in possession of Scotland, may encourage France to put him in Possession of England also.' Even without Charles Edward's efforts to topple the House of Hanover, government fears of a renewed French invasion attempt had heightened by the late summer of 1745. The French armies in Flanders had piled success on top of success, with victory over the allies (commanded by the Duke of Cumberland) at Fontenoy being rapidly followed by the capture of the strategic towns of Ghent, Bruges and Ostend. England, like Scotland, was denuded of troops at the time, and Pelham informed Henry Fox that 'we have not left troops enough in this country to mount guard at the royal palaces, nor to quell an insurrection or smuggling party of one hundred men'. Charles Edward's defeat of Cope meant that England was now menaced on two fronts; unless the government responded quickly and decisively to this new threat then George II's crown would indeed be, as Newcastle himself owned, 'in the utmost danger'.

But the unity of purpose required to ensure quick and decisive action was conspicuously lacking in government circles. The cabinet was split between those who backed the Pelhams' view that troops needed to be withdrawn from Flanders to deal with the deepening crisis at home, and the supporters of Carteret who, despite his resignation from government in November 1744, still wielded considerable influence over the king. This latter group, which included Tweeddale, argued that removing troops from Europe when France was very much in the ascendancy would serve only to weaken the resolve and military capacity of Britain's Continental allies. The situation was summed up by Andrew Mitchell, who complained of a 'divided and diffident Ministry; the rage of Party still so strong, that they are more animated against each other than against the common enemy'.

Paradoxically, the defeat at Prestonpans brought some succour to the Pelhams, since the news finally persuaded the waverers to come round to their way of thinking. Even George II, who had earlier been extremely reluctant to bring back troops from the Continent, was now convinced that the Jacobites posed the more immediate threat. This is not to say that measures had not already been taken to reinforce the troops then stationed in Britain, but rather that Prestonpans hastened the process. On 27 August the Dutch had agreed to send 6000 of their troops to Scotland at the request of the British government, under the terms of a defensive treaty which existed between the two nations. These men were part of the garrison of Tournai which had surrendered to the French in June, and the terms of their capitulation stipulated that the Dutch troops were not to be employed against France or her allies until 1 January 1747. The French—not surprisingly—immediately protested that sending the 6000 men to Scotland was in direct contravention of these terms. The Dutch answered that they were merely responding to a request for help to put down an internal rebellion which should be of no concern to France, particularly as France had previously declared that she 'had no Hand in the Project of the Pretender'; moreover, James was not yet 'looked upon, nor known to be an Ally of that Crown'. The Abbé de la Ville, who made the protest, was said to have been 'exceedingly nettled and disconcerted by this answer'. The diplomatic row between the two countries rumbled on until December, when Lord John Drummond's arrival in Scotland with troops serving in the French army finally forced the Dutch to comply with French demands. The 6000 Dutch troops were thus never actively engaged at any stage of the rising.

But it was British troops that were needed most of all. Even before Prestonpans, ten battalions of infantry under the command of Sir John Ligonier had been ordered to return to Britain, and these forces disembarked at Gravesend on 23 September. On 26 September Cumberland was ordered to send over a further eight battalions and nine squadrons of cavalry from Flanders, while additional reinforcements were dispatched from Ireland. These troops, together with the six thousand or so men stationed in England at the start of the rising, made up a formidable force, which was augmented by the militia and a number of regiments raised by loyal Whig landowners.

The regular troops were divided into three army groups whose disposition reflected the strategic dilemma facing the government. France was still seen as the major threat, and for this reason a 'very considerable force' remained in the south-east, close to London, 'for the defence and security of the

William Augustus, Duke of Cumberland (1721-1765) was younger than Prince Charles by a few months, but on entering the British army was promoted major-general in 1742, lieutenant-general in 1743 and captain-general in 1745. These posts reflected his royal status rather than his abilities, but he did have more experience as a soldier than Prince Charles, and enjoyed the considerable advantage of being surrounded by vastly-experienced general officers. (Scottish National Portrait Gallery)

Capital, and for the preservation of peace in these parts'. But with the disintegration of Cope's army, troops also had to be sent north to prevent Charles Edward from occupying northern England unopposed, and so a force of some eight to ten thousand men, under the aged Marshall Wade, was sent north to Newcastle. The third force, to be commanded by Ligonier, was eventually to move towards Lancashire in case the Jacobites should somehow manage to defeat or avoid Wade.

It was not only in England that preparations were being made to frustrate the rising. In the Highlands, Lord President Forbes was doing his utmost to prevent the uncommitted clans from joining Charles Edward. In this he was only partially successful: the Macphersons of Cluny, some of the Macintoshes under 'Colonel Anne' (wife of the laird, who himself remained loyal to the government), and, eventually, the Frasers under Lovat's eldest son, Simon, were to join the prince. The government had provided Forbes with the means to secure the loyalty of these clans by sending down twenty blank commissions 'to be distributed among the well-affected clans as your Lordship shall think proper'. In all, eighteen independent companies were raised by Forbes, the commissions being handed out to suitable persons recommended by the chiefs of clans Munro, Sutherland, Mackay, Grant, Ross, Macleods of Skye and Assynt, Mackenzies of Kintail and Lewis and Macdonalds of Skye. But Forbes was plagued by a lack of both arms and money, and recruiting went slowly; only two companies were completed before the end of October, the others taking considerably longer. The command of these companies was given to John Campbell, 4th Earl of Loudoun, who arrived at Inverness on 11 October accompanied by 150 men from his own regiment (most of the rest having been captured at Prestonpans). Four nights later, Forbes's residence, Culloden House, was attacked by a party of Frasers under James Fraser of Foyers, with orders to seize Forbes and take him into custody. The raid was beaten off, although some sixty sheep and twenty-nine cattle were stolen. Lovat later protested his innocence, claiming that the raid had been carried out by renegades and promising to return the livestock to Forbes if and when they were recovered. Forbes, in a vain attempt to keep Lovat sweet, pretended to accept his version of events, but proof of Lovat's complicity came with Murray of Broughton's assertion that Lovat later blamed the débâcle on the warrant issued by Charles which prevented him from taking Forbes 'dead or alive', resulting in his men being 'obliged to make a shameful retreat inconsistent with the honour of his Clan'!

During the six weeks that the Jacobites remained in Edinburgh, recruiting men and requisitioning supplies, the government consolidated and stabilised the military situation both in England and, with the help of Forbes, in northern Scotland. Now Charles would have to watch his back if he went south, and any French invasion would encounter far stiffer resistance than would have been the case some weeks earlier. Apprehension and fear still prevailed south of the border, but much had been done to redress the balance, as Charles was soon to discover.

5 INVASION

And tho' there were three regular Armies in England, each of them more numerous than they...if these Armies had been removed, eight Millions of People must have been subdued and reduced to Slavery by five Thousand, the bravest, but still the most worthless amongst them.
(DAVID HUME, 'A TRUE ACCOUNT OF THE BEHAVIOUR AND CONDUCT OF ARCHIBALD STEWART, ESQ., LATE LORD PROVOST OF EDINBURGH', 1748)

ON 31 October 1745 the Jacobite army left its billets in and around Edinburgh to muster at Dalkeith. Although its destination was Carlisle, few knew this and no effort was made to dispel the impression that it was marching to confront Marshal Wade in Northumberland. There was a delay at Dalkeith following reports of pro-Hanoverian demonstrations at Perth and Dundee on the occasion of the king's birthday (30 October). Orders were dispatched north and the army moved off in two columns, but such unwelcome news no doubt set minds working afresh on the wisdom of the decision taken by the council of war. The main body consisted of the so-called Lowland regiments (the Atholl Brigade, Perth's, Ogilvy's, Glenbucket's and Roy Stewart's), plus the baggage and artillery. Commanded by the Dukes of Atholl and Perth, it took a direct route to the south via Peebles and Moffat. Prince Charles and Lord George

Pinkie House, Musselburgh. Prince Charles rested at Pinkie House after the battle of Prestonpans, and again on leaving Edinburgh to begin the invasion of England. (By kind permission of Loretto School)

67

Lauder Castle

Thirlestane Castle, Lauder, from John Slezer's Theatrum Scotiae. *Prince Charles spent a night at the Earl of Lauderdale's castle on his journey south to the English border. (National Library of Scotland)*

Field Marshal George Wade (1673-1748), former commander-in-chief in Scotland. In the 1720s Wade had begun supervising the construction of the 'Chain' of forts, linked by specially cut roads, which were designed to allow government forces to pacify the Highlands. By 1745, his age and his ill-health prevented him carrying out his duties effectively — a common problem in the army, as seniority stemmed from length of service. (Scottish National Portrait Gallery)

Murray, accompanied by Elcho's Lifeguards and the clan or Highland regiments, set out on the Kelso road as if making for Newcastle, and then swung south to Jedburgh. Charles endeared himself to the rough clansmen by leading his column on foot the whole way, dressed like them in a plaid, refusing to mount even to ford rivers. His column crossed the River Esk into England on 8 November and reunited with the other column on the following day. The feint succeeded in keeping Marshal Wade on the defensive in Newcastle while the army penetrated into the north-west and began the siege of Carlisle which, as the Chevalier de Johnstone described it, seemed much more promising as a first foothold in England:

> Carlisle, a considerable town, and capital of the county of Cumberland is only about a league and a half distant from the borders of Scotland...It is surrounded by walls flanked with towers, and a fosse, and contains a castle well furnished with artillery, and defended by a garrison of invalids. This castle was formerly a place of considerable strength; but at present its walls, like those of the town, are falling from age into decay. We opened our trenches before this place, under the orders of the Duke of Perth, on the night of the 10th of November.

In fact the normal garrison of Carlisle was supplemented by just over 200 local militia and thirty-eight of Cope's regulars who had fled there. The garrison had managed to obtain extra cannon from Whitehaven shortly before, and the magistrates even congratulated themselves on their preparations when it became clear that the siege was being suspended almost immediately after earthworks were opened. The Jacobites had received a report that Marshal Wade was attempting to march across the Pennines to give them battle. Although it had been Lord George Murray's intention to avoid confronting Wade if possible, most of the army decamped to

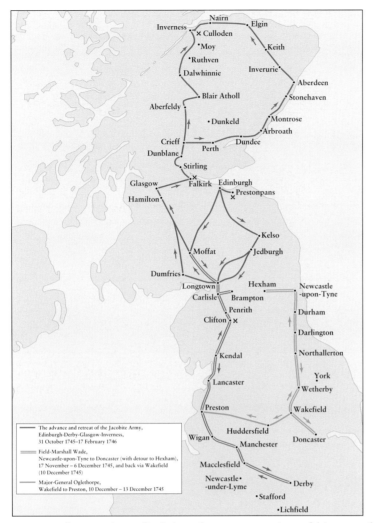

The legend on the map reads:

The advance and retreat of the Jacobite Army,
Edinburgh-Derby-Glasgow-Inverness,
31 October 1745–17 February 1746

Field-Marshall Wade,
Newcastle-upon-Tyne to Doncaster (with detour to Hexham),
17 November – 6 December 1745, and back via Wakefield
(10 December 1745)

Major-General Oglethorpe,
Wakefield to Preston, 10 December – 13 December 1745

The Jacobites' invasion of England and retreat north, October 1745-February 1746.

Brampton to meet him, only to find that there was no sign of his army being on the move. Wade was still making preparations at Newcastle and, with heavy snow certain to impede any immediate attempt to relieve Carlisle, the Jacobites returned to resume their siege on the 13th.

They reappeared at Carlisle and opened batteries. They had only light artillery available, but it was enough to demoralise the militia and the townspeople. Against the advice of the commanding officer, Lieutenant-Colonel Durand, they drew the same conclusion as their besiegers, that Wade would probably not arrive in time to save them, and on the 14th they pressed Durand to surrender. He reluctantly agreed to surrender the town only, but Charles, in the light of events at Edinburgh, refused to accept this, insisting on the surrender of both town and castle. Durand capitulated on the 15th, although he first obtained a paper signed by the magistrates exonerating him from any blame in the affair. The prince rode into Carlisle in triumph on the 17th, by which time Wade had been on the road for two days and had only reached Hexham.

No-one in Carlisle knew it, since its reported strength of more than 10,000 made it seem a formidable force, but Wade's army was in poor

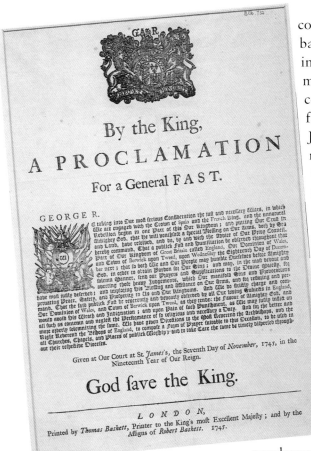

By the King,

A PROCLAMATION

For a General FAST.

GEORGE R.

Royal Proclamation for a General Fast in England and Wales, on Wednesday 18 December 1745: 'that so both We and Our People may humble Ourselves before Almighty God, in order to obtain Pardon for Our Sins...' (National Library of Scotland, Blk.732)

condition: weakened by dysentery and seasickness, badly equipped, starved and driven to insubordination (particularly the foreign mercenaries who made up more than half the command). More men died on the short journey from Newcastle to Hexham and back than the Jacobites were to lose on their 500 mile round march into England. Many simply froze to death. On hearing that Carlisle had already fallen, Wade returned to his camp with over 1000 men sick. If the Jacobites had been better informed of Wade's problems (many of which can be traced to his meanness with money) they might have taken a completely different view of their position. The same can also be said of those viewing events in the north of England from London drawing-rooms.

The unimpeded march from Edinburgh and the capture of Carlisle lifted the spirits of many in the army, and underlined what an advantage the superior mobility (and hardiness) of its irregular troops was to its commanders, when compared to the ponderous movements of regular forces. More than anything else, it was the Jacobite army's capacity for rapid movement which disconcerted its opponents, both on the battlefield and off it. According to the Chevalier de Johnstone:

> The principal object in the disposition of our marches, was to keep the English always in a state of uncertainty with regard to our movements, the towns to which we intended to go, and the roads we meant to take. Continually baffled by our manoeuvres, they were obliged to remain inactive till they could learn our real object, by the reunion of our columns, by which they lost a great deal of time.

The Jacobites, however, also had their problems. The commanders were even more divided about the expedition's objectives now that they had left Scotland behind. Bad news followed them of loyal militias being raised at Glasgow, Stirling, Paisley and Dumfries. This was capped by the deflating news that Edinburgh had been re-occupied by government troops, amid general rejoicing, the same week. The march from Edinburgh had also amply demonstrated some of the drawbacks of having irregular troops to command. Large numbers of men had deserted on the road, which meant the army's total strength was now around 5000. In addition, on arrival, Lord George Murray learned that most of the baggage, including the tents, had been 'lost', that is to say, it had been taken by the country people when not properly guarded. This meant that the army would in future have to be quartered in towns. To make things worse, the mutual personal dislike of Prince Charles and Lord George Murray became clearer after the surrender of Carlisle.

Admitting that he knew little about siegecraft, Lord George had allowed his fellow general, the Duke of Perth, to direct the siege; but when Perth was given the honour of accepting the town's surrender without reference to himself, he exploded. He stressed the stupidity of the prince's decision: to have a Roman Catholic take the surrender of the first English town to be captured was handing the Whigs a propaganda coup. He resigned his commission, and offered Charles his services as an ordinary volunteer. Charles accepted, unaware that the leaders of the clan regiments had already sided with Lord George. The invasion was threatened with crisis. In reality, the general was incensed at the prince's habit of taking advice from a kitchen-cabinet (as he saw it) of junior officers and inferior men, foremost among whom was his secretary, John Murray of Broughton. James Maxwell of Kirkconnell (and others) later claimed that Murray of Broughton sought to exploit his prior acquaintance with the prince and 'from the beginning aimed at nothing less than the whole direction and management of every thing'. As his main rival, Lord George suffered most from the fact that 'All those Gentlemen that joined the Prince after [John] Murray were made known under the character he thought fit to give them…' Lord George would have liked the secretary put out, not the Duke of Perth, but he was placated somewhat when friends of the duke persuaded the younger, more flexible man to cede rank to him for the good of the cause. Although Charles was thus forced to reinstate Lord George and make him sole field commander, he did so with an ill-will. Thereafter — and quite ominously — they preferred to avoid one another.

Tension permeated the council of war called at Carlisle on 18 November. Murray of Broughton told the council that a shortage of money meant that remaining at Carlisle was not an option. Lord George Murray and his supporters spoke out: they were for a return to Scotland. At this point the prince prompted the Marquis d'Eguilles to reveal his instructions from Louis XV. These made it clear that the French were not prepared to intervene until they had had a chance to gauge the support from Jacobites in England. This meant marching further south into the supposedly sympathetic county of Lancashire. The clan leaders were forced to agree. A letter was sent to Lord Strathallan at Perth ordering him to bring what troops he had collected to England as reinforcements.

*****

The army left Carlisle in two columns. One, led by Elcho's Guards and commanded by Lord George, set out a day ahead of the other so that both could use the same quarters. The prince's column followed, reaching Penrith on 21 November, Kendal on the 23rd and Lancaster on the 25th, and resting on the other days. The two columns joined again at Preston and Lord George requested a council meeting. The reason was obvious, given that Preston had unhappy associations for the Scots in the light of their defeats there in 1648 and 1715. The army had met little opposition except for some sabotage to roads and bridges, but it had failed to attract any real support. While Whig observers had lamented the danger from 'the indifferency and lukewarmness of the many', the invaders were finding that this cut both ways. However, Jacobite scouts placed Marshal Wade's army still in or near Newcastle, and, as far as was known, the army under Sir John Ligonier was too far to the south to present an immediate threat. This left the sceptics room to be persuaded that at Manchester the English Jacobites would come forward in numbers. The basis for this was flimsy. The council was unaware that the prince had not troubled to make use of the Jacobite agents who did exist in England (who were still reporting to Paris), or that the very few letters he sent ahead of him to leading Jacobite sympathisers were being intercepted.

The reaction of the local inhabitants as the army marched south is described by Lord Elcho:

> The road betwixt Preston and Wigan was crouded with people standing at their doors to see the army go by, and they generaly all that days march profes'd to wish the Princes army Success, but if arms was offer'd to them and they were desir'd to Go along with the army they all declined, and Said they did not Understand fighting…[At Manchester] every body was astonish'd to find that all that was to join was about 200 Common fellows who it seems had no subsistance…Their was one or two Gentlemen and about 15 or 20…merchants likewise joined, the Prince formed them into a Regiment which was Called the Manchester regiment and gave the command of it to Mr Townly a Roman Catholick. The Prince was so far deceived with…bonfires and ringing of bells (which they used to own themselves they did out of fear of being ill Used) that he thought himself sure of Success, and his Conversation that night at Table was, in what Manner he should enter London, on horseback or a-foot, and in what dress.

It was borne in on the government that the militias were melting away and that, because of the state of the roads, the cavalry would be unable to halt the rebels in southern Lancashire. London looked like their objective but it was not clear where in the Midlands to send forces to intercept them. Until he reached Derby, the prince enjoyed the full benefit of the opportunity thrown up by his impetuosity. Precisely because little was concerted ahead of his line of march, there was little to leak out. But his lack of a definite plan placed him in a cleft stick: not only the government was anxiously wondering if he was acting according to some carefully laid scheme, Jacobites were too.

When Sir John Ligonier fell ill, the command of the government army in the Midlands was taken over by the Duke of Cumberland, who had returned from Flanders in mid-October. Hearing rumours mentioning Wales, which the Scots had spread deliberately, the duke moved his headquarters from Lichfield to Stafford. When he received reports of a large body of men moving quickly from Macclesfield to Congleton on 2 December he became convinced that the Jacobites were heading for Wales. He selected a battle site at Stone to cut them off and sent orders for his regiments to concentrate there. The body he thought was the main Jacobite army was in fact a force of 1200 men led by Lord George Murray, which doubled back and rejoined the main column of the prince's army on 3 December. They reached Leek the same day and Derby on 4 December. The Duke of Cumberland realized his mistake and got to Stafford on the 4th, but Derby and Stafford are about the same distance from London and the Jacobites could move more quickly. Marshal Wade was several days' march behind both of them, at Wetherby. A feint had worked once again. This time the core of the British army had been given the slip.

In its December issue, the *Gentleman's Magazine* printed a letter giving a vivid account of the Highland army at Derby to its readers:

> The van-guard rode into town, consisting of about 30 men, cloath'd in blue, fac'd with red; most of them had on scarlet waistcoats with gold lace, and being likely men made a good appearance. They were drawn up in the market-place, and sat on horseback 2 or 3 hours; at the same time the bells were rung, and several bonfires made, to prevent any resentment

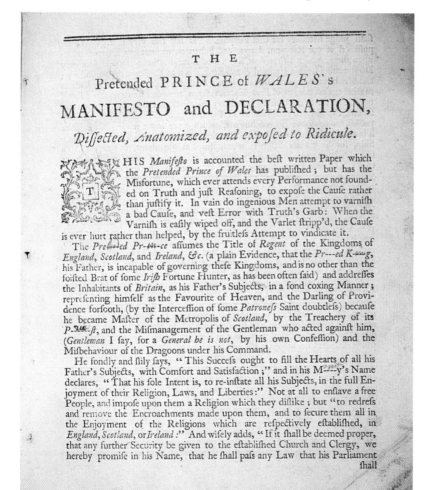

A Whig riposte to Prince Charles's Declaration of 14 October 1745. (National Library of Scotland, Ry.1.5.249)

from them…About 3 in the afternoon lord *Elcho*, with the life-guards, and many of their chiefs also arriv'd on horseback to the number of about 150, most of them cloathed as above; these made a fine show, being the flower of their army: soon after their main body also march'd into town in tolerable order, six or eight a-breast, with about 8 standards, most of them white flags and a red cross. They had several bag-pipers, who play'd as they march'd along; they appear'd in general to answer the description we have all along had of them, *viz.* most of their main body a parcel of shabby, lousy, pitiful-look'd fellows, mix'd up with old men and boys; dress'd in dirty plaids, and as dirty shirts, without breeches, and wore their stockings made of plaid, not much above half way up their legs, and some without shoes, or next to none, and numbers of them so fatigu'd with their long march, that they really commanded our pity more than fear…Being refresh'd with a night's rest, they were very alert the next day, running about from one shop to another, to buy, or rather steal, tradesmen's goods.

The day in question was, of course, 5 December and it was in an oak-panelled room in Exeter House, while clansmen were scouring the streets of Derby to find cutlers to sharpen their swords for a battle, that the decision was taken to retreat to Scotland.

The prince met his officers, blithely assuming that they were to discuss how they would get to London. Like the clansmen outside, he was confident in the extreme and in no mood to dwell on obstacles, but the majority of the council did not share his optimism. Lord George Murray spoke for the colonels of the clan regiments. He made it plain that they were against any march to London. His reasons were the same as they had been at Carlisle, at Preston, and at Manchester — only now, he said, they were surrounded by 30,000 men in three armies (a figure puffed up by a government agent they had come across). To reach the capital, in the best possible case, they would have to defeat an army twice the size of their own in pitched battle and expect to suffer high casualties. They would then have to disperse the local militia, and their ultimate fate would depend upon the disposition of a mob in a city of a million people where there was believed to be growing panic. The prince was being swayed by his Irish advisers who, as officers in the pay of France, could expect to be ransomed if captured; in the event of losing a battle, the Scots could expect only the fate of traitors; the prince himself would certainly be taken. Lord Elcho recalled:

> Lord George concluded by Saying that the Scots army had done their part, that they Came into England at the Princes request, to join his English friends, and to give them Courage by their appearance to take arms and declare for him publickly as they had done, or to join the French if they had Landed; but as none of these things had happened, that certainly 4500 Scots had never thought of putting a King upon the English throne by themselves. So he Said his Opinion was they Should go back and join their friends in Scotland, and live and die with them.

Lord John Drummond, 4th (titular) Duke of Perth (1714-1747), by Domenico Dupra. (Scottish National Portrait Gallery)

The prince was flabbergasted. His disclosure of the news that Lord John Drummond had landed at Montrose with around 800 men, and ten times that number expected to follow, had the opposite effect on his officers to the one he intended: the lords and chiefs interpreted it as the best possible reason to step back from the peril they were in through want of numbers. When he realized that all his arguments were carrying no weight in the council and its decision was not going to be reversed, the prince's temper snapped completely: 'You ruin, abandon and betray me if you don't march on!' he flung at them. It was in vain. He had stretched his personal credibility too far.

*****

With the benefit of hindsight it is possible to say that, from the military point of view, the position of the Jacobites at Derby was much better than they supposed. The only force which stood between the invaders and the capital was the large militia assembled on Finchley Common. Like the Edinburgh militia, it was a ramshackle body of enthusiasts, strengthened this time by a few regiments of experienced regulars. But in London not much was expected from it. Many people believed that an attack was imminent. Bills were pasted up at night prophesying it, and soldiers were posted in the main streets and squares to keep order. There was a run on the Bank of England (which preserved its stock by issuing it in sixpences to its own agents, who then returned it by a back door, thus keeping the public at bay). Those who could packed their valuables and prepared to leave. The king was said to have his yachts moored in readiness at Tower Quay, and the Duke of Newcastle was rumoured to be contemplating a switch of allegiance. Support for the prince was growing in the shires. Some leading Welsh and English Jacobites had finally been encouraged to raise men, and sent messages to the prince telling him that they were moving to his aid. (Unfortunately the messenger arrived at Derby only after the retreat had begun.) The Hanoverian regime was teetering; a defeat in the field followed by seizure of the Treasury — cutting off the army and navy's finance — might have given the push needed to topple it. All of this was lost on the council. They saw only the danger in their military situation and interpreted the lack of support they had met as hostility. As the historian A. J. Youngson has pointed out, *in their actual state of mind* they could have reached no other decision.

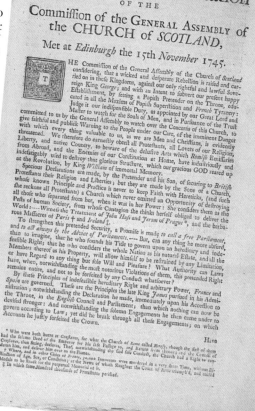

While the Prince's army was in England, government forces regained control of Edinburgh. The General Assembly of the Church of Scotland was quick to resume its condemnation of the 'wicked and desperate Rebellion'. (National Library of Scotland; on loan to the Scottish National Portrait Gallery)

*****

The following morning, Friday 6 December, which was to achieve lasting notoriety in Jacobite annals as 'Black Friday', the Highland army began its long retreat. The *Gentleman's Magazine* described their going:

> Early on Friday morning their drums beat to arms, and their bag-pipers play'd about the town; no one then knowing their route, but most people imagined they would march to *Loughborough* for *London*, their advance-guard having secured the pass at *Swarkston* bridge: however; we were soon undeceived, by their precipitate retreat the same road they came, marching off about 7 o'clock in the morning...their chiefs seeming much confus'd, and all in a great hurry; some of their men left their horses, swords, pistols, targets, shot, powder, bullets, and other odd things behind them, where they quarter'd; a plain proof of their confusion. Their pretended prince mounted upon a black horse, (said to be the brave Col. *Gardner*'s) left his lodgings about 9 o' clock.

The Jacobite army was retreating, literally and metaphorically in the dark. Once again deceit was practised to gain the maximum advantage. Cavalry were sent out of Derby on the London road, but only to skirt the town and head north again. The Jacobite infantry were similarly deluded, as Maxwell of Kirkconnell relates:

> Powder and ball were distributed as before an action, and it was insinuated that Wade was at hand, and they were going to fight him; but when the soldiers found themselves on the road to Ashborn, they began to suspect the truth, and seemed extremely dejected...[A]nother artifice was thought of to amuse them: It was given out that the reinforcements expected from Scotland were on the road, and had already entered England; that Wade was endeavouring to intercept them, and the Prince was marching to their relief; that as soon as they had joined him, he would resume his march to London...The hopes of returning immediately made them somewhat easy under their present disappointment, but still all was sullen and silent that whole day.

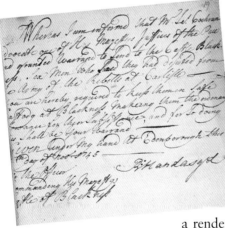

A warrant from General Roger Handasyd, commander at Edinburgh, to the officer commanding Blackness Castle, to detain and subsist six Jacobite deserters, 29 November 1745. (National Library of Scotland, MS.288, f.19)

One thing was clear however. When the government learnt that Prince Charles had turned back they realised at once that the rebels were not acting in concert with the French. The prospect of a rendezvous with French regulars, perhaps commanded by Marshal Saxe, the most admired and feared general in Europe at the time, had filled the Whig imagination with dread. But the clan leaders never appreciated the effect on their opponents' morale of expecting to fight on two fronts at once. Their decision to retreat showed that there was no Popish Plot for a joint invasion: that Charles was either acting alone or — perhaps unwittingly — creating a diversion for a French thrust against the Netherlands. It was the turning point in the conflict. Although the threat of a French invasion remained, there was a widespread feeling that when the Jacobites marched out of Derby the initiative in the struggle passed to the government for the

The March of the Guards to Finchley *(1750) by William Hogarth. Like a number of familiar representations of the '45, this scene was painted some years after the rebellion. (National Library of Scotland; on loan to the Scottish National Portrait Gallery)*

first time. The undeclared war would continue for another five months — and the reprisals for longer — but the *coup d'état* was at an end: it had failed. As Horace Walpole put it, 'No one is afraid of a rebellion that runs away'.

Hermann Maurice (Moritz), Count of Saxony, Marshal of France (1696-1750) by Maurice Quentin de La Tour. In the first half of the eighteenth century, Saxe eclipsed all his rivals as a strategist, defeating the Duke of Cumberland in three successive battles during the War of the Austrian Succession. (The Royal Collection© Her Majesty Queen Elizabeth II)

Caricature of the Duke of Cumberland (c1746-50), by his aid-de-camp, George, 4th Viscount and 1st Marquess Townshend. (By courtesy of the National Portrait Gallery, London)

*****

With Lord George in command of the rearguard, the Jacobite army retraced its steps, reaching Macclesfield on 8 December. The Duke of Cumberland needed to rest and regroup his forces whatever happened, but he was still anticipating a move south two days after the rebels had begun their retreat. He assumed that Wade would draw a net around the rebels if they returned north; in fact the marshal was further away than he expected. This meant that the rebels had slightly more than two days' start when Cumberland's cavalry and a thousand infantry mounted on borrowed horses left Meriden Common on 8 December. This was the sort of advantage that Lord George Murray had counted on when he counselled a retreat. He reckoned that if the army could cross the Ribble at Preston ahead of the pursuit there was a good chance of escaping altogether. He knew that the uplands of the north-western counties, with their walled fields and roads, would make it difficult for a large force to close with them and force a battle. He was aware that if Marshal Wade guessed their intentions correctly he could cross the Pennines and confront them in central Lancashire — if necessary the Jacobites were prepared to fight their way through one army. He was also gambling that the army would cope if the militias rose and broke the roads and bridges ahead of their line of march. That news of an abortive expedition led by the Duc de Richelieu and Charles's younger brother Henry Stuart, planned for the third week of December, would twice halt the pursuers, he could hardly have counted on.

On the return journey the Jacobite army met with open hostility, the result of the fear, confusion and anger provoked by the rebellion. The fearful state of many of the troops showed itself in poorer discipline. In response to attacks there were some killings and not a few robberies; a few men mutinied and some deserted. The grisly fate that absconders suffered in unsympathetic hands clearly showed that it was safer to stick with the body of the army. Although it was calculated the rugged clansmen could cover nearly three times the distance in a day that regular infantry could manage, there were cavalry regiments in their rear, and in May 1745 newspapers had reported the feat of a Huntingdonshire man who, for a wager, had ridden more than 200 miles in just over twelve hours. Francis Townley, for one, slept with guards on his door, so great was his fear that the Duke of Cumberland would catch up with them. In fact, their pursuers did manage a considerable feat of horsemanship, at one stage covering around 100 miles in three days on snow-bound roads. Even aided by unforeseen advantages, the Jacobites were to be caught and harried within a week of leaving Derby.

On 9 December they arrived at Manchester where they were met by a violent mob. A show of force quelled the opposition and a fine of £2500 was exacted as punishment. But what was worse, in view of the need for haste, was that Prince Charles was clearly dragging his feet. With childish petulance he had been prevaricating at every opportunity; now he stood on his dignity and insisted on remaining in the town a full day. No part of him wanted to retreat back into Scotland and his natural stubbornness, which had previously been a positive force on the expedition, turned demon after Derby. In his blackest moods, brooding over how he had been frustrated, he conveyed the impression that he did not care if the army was destroyed. Forcing his commanders to observe the form of an orderly withdrawal rather than a rapid retreat was his way of thwarting them, and is evidence of deep anger towards his officers. He had a settled policy of humaneness towards prisoners, but on the retreat out of England, when clemency for spies and saboteurs was misplaced, he insisted on this magnanimity, knowing that it jeopardised the army's safety. His enemy, Cumberland, had no such inhibitions with regard to stragglers from the rebel army. '[A]s they have so many of our prisoners in their hands,' he wrote to the Duke of Newcastle, 'I did not care to put them to death. But I have encouraged the country people to do it.'

Prince Henry Stuart as a young man. (National Library of Scotland; on loan to the Scottish National Portrait Gallery)

*****

On 10 December, faced with supply problems, Marshal Wade held a council of war at Wakefield. The infantry regiments would retire to Newcastle, while Major-General Oglethorpe was to command a cavalry detachment to cross the Pennines and link up with the duke's forces. Oglethorpe, however, was hampered by infantry quartered along his route, and the Jacobites reached Wigan on the 10th and Preston on 11 December. Again they met trouble and again they halted. Fears were expressed to the prince that the army would break up once it reached Scotland. To forestall this, the Duke of Perth and the Marquis d'Eguilles proposed defending Preston and using it as a base, possibly even going into winter quarters until reinforced. The idea was rejected by the other commanders, but Perth was sent north with a strong party to hasten Lords Strathallan and Drummond.

On 13 December, while the main body was making for Lancaster, the rearguard skirmished with Oglethorpe's scouts at Garstang. Elcho writes that 'At Supper at Lancaster the Prince talk'd much about retiring so fast, and said it was a Shame to go so fast before the son of an *Usurper*, and that he Would stay at Lancaster'. The following morning Lord George Murray went with Lochiel and O'Sullivan to select a battlefield, only to find when they returned that the prince had opted to move on. Murray asked for the heavy baggage and the artillery in his charge to be abandoned to speed their progress, but the prince refused. According to Kirkconnell, 'the Prince was positive not to leave a single piece of his cannon; he would rather fight both their armies than give such an argument of fear and weakness'. This decision turned the following few days into a nightmare for the Glengarry regiment, which was then acting as the rearguard. The Duke of Newcastle had sent orders to halt Cumberland when the threat of a French invasion seemed greatest, on 12 December. His orders reached Wigan on the 14th and Cumberland recalled Oglethorpe, unaware that he was on the Jacobites' heels. The Jacobites benefited from the delay, but it became clear by the 14th that the invasion had been postponed. Meanwhile, Cumberland sent instructions ahead to the lord lieutenants to raise the militia against the rebels. As a result the Duke of Perth's party was ambushed near Shap and was driven back to Kendal in confusion. The main body and the rearguard encountered hostility in the town itself. Some soldiers killed civilians and looted property in reprisal. Lord George lost four horses, and, as they left, the rearguard was fired on by a group led by a parson.

The Cumbrian hills meant safety for the main body of the army, which pushed on to Penrith. Adrift and slowed to a crawl, the rearguard was more vulnerable to attack. On the 16th, hampered by the weather, illness, a shortage of food and lack of proper carts, it was reduced to manhandling equipment across rivers and through deep mud, with officers joining in. At night the regiment sheltered at a farm steading. On 17 December 200 cannon balls were carried uphill to Shap in plaids, with each willing man being paid sixpence, but a quantity of powder had to be spoiled with water when some carts broke. At Shap, where they ate the last of their provisions, they found themselves burdened with more equipment. The following morning, mounted parties appeared in the surrounding hills and began to shadow them. These moved in close enough to require a screen of forty men to fan out behind the column to ward them off. Shortly after, a body of horsemen appeared on the Penrith road. Bidden by a junior Irish officer, the Glengarry men drew their weapons and gave chase, quickly scattering the nervous militia, but also exposing the baggage train. Lord George realised that the tactic of hastening ahead of the pursuers had run its course: the rearguard was close to being surrounded. Now only a decisive check to the enemy would keep it intact. The baggage was hurried on through Clifton to Penrith to join the main army, while the rearguard attempted to run down militia patrols near Lowther Hall. A captured footman and an officer yielded information that Cumberland was nearby with up to 4000 cavalry. Although this was suspected to be an overestimate, a request for reinforcements was sent to Penrith, while the Glengarry regiment and John Roy Stewart's assembled at Clifton.

The prince would not send a large force back to Clifton because he thought that the rearguard was only confronting militia, but, when they heard the news, the Macphersons and Ardshiel's men set off at speed. They arrived to find their comrades under sporadic fire from a party of 500 dragoons which had dismounted and penetrated the outskirts of the village some way ahead of their main body. The Highlanders had the advantage of being much less visible in the gathering dusk and used it to line the hedges while drawing the enemy into a pocket. At the shout of 'Claymore!' they cut their way through the thickets, fired a volley and fell on the cavalrymen. They quickly forced them back, despite breaking a number of swords on armour, and the attack was soon called off — although some Macphersons who failed to hear the order were captured following up. Under cover of darkness the four regiments reformed and hurried on to Penrith. Having lost about forty men in the skirmish (the last 'battle' on English soil), the Duke of Cumberland chose not to pursue them.

The following day, the army marched to Carlisle where, in the eyes of his detractors, Prince Charles capped the folly he had shown hitherto. On O'Sullivan's advice, he insisted that Carlisle be left garrisoned so that the army could march into England again once it was reinforced. The Manchester regiment made up the core of about 300 men selected for this duty. Most officers believed that blowing up the fortifications would have achieved the same object but, not expecting to see Carlisle again for the most part, few said as much. On 20 December the rest of the army marched to the border and crossed the flooded Esk in ranks abreast. Once on the Scottish bank they lit fires and danced themselves dry to the skirl of pipes. The poverty of the countryside in winter prevented an immediate incursion by cavalry, so the Duke of Cumberland sent to Whitehaven for cannon and then laid siege to Carlisle for the second time in two months.

On the same day as the skirmish at Clifton, news of the Jacobite retreat from Derby was received in France, where an invasion force of 15,000 men was being assembled under Louis' favourite, the Duc de Richelieu. He was

Admiral Edward Vernon (1684-1757) by Charles Philips. Vernon's victory at the battle of Porto Bello in 1739 turned him into a popular hero, and despite failure in three subsequent actions he was made an Admiral in 1745. His success in deterring the French invasion attempt of 1745/6 was short-lived: later in 1746 he was cashiered for speaking out against government policy. (National Maritime Museum, London)

relishing promotion on the strength of an easy victory, even if it meant putting up with the company of Henry Stuart, whom he found excessively pious, but when the possibility of catching British forces in a pincer movement disappeared, so did some of Richelieu's enthusiasm for the proposed expedition. He now began to appreciate the winter storms, and Admiral Vernon's waiting fleet, for what they turned out in fact to be: formidable obstacles.

6 FALKIRK

COPE would not *cope*,
Nor WADE *wade* through the snow,
Nor HAWLEY *haul* his cannon to the foe.

(JACOBITE VERSE)

THE Jacobites' retreat into Scotland, through 'enemy' territory, in terrible weather, with the loss of only forty-odd men, was one of the more remarkable forced marches in military history. But they were now in the Presbyterian south-west of Scotland, which, with Argyllshire, was the part of the country most hostile to them. Marching north in two columns, they were unwelcome guests at a number of towns and ducal seats. These included Dumfries, which was fined for the robbery of the army's baggage on the way south, and Drumlanrig Castle, the residence of the Duke of Queensberry, where portraits of the Protestant 'usurpers' were slashed with swords. Departing from previous practice, the officers were reluctant to pay for their quarters — a pointed mark of their displeasure since the prince was not at this stage short of funds: the army had sustained itself in England by seizures and exactions. The prince enjoyed a holiday at Christmas, hunting in the Duke of Hamilton's park. There was little goodwill lost between his army and the local inhabitants however. The previous autumn, Macdonald of Kinlochmoidart had been detained in the vicinity of Lesmahagow and handed over to the authorities. Several houses were looted and burned in the search for culprits. The town of Hamilton too seems to have suffered:

[W]e felt the Effects of an undisciplin'd ungovernable Army of Highland Robbers, who took no more Notice of their nominal Prince, or Commanders, than a Pack of ill-bred Hounds. The Provisions, Ale and Spirits, beginning to run short in the Town, they threatened the People with Death, or the burning their Houses, unless such Victuals and Drink were got as they call'd for…While here, they strip'd the People of their Shoes upon the Street, and took what they thought proper for them, refusing to be hinder'd by any of their Officers. There was not any of this Rabble, but what were possess'd of Plenty of Gold, even the smallest Boys, and nakedest Whores. We were freed from these troublesome Neighbours

A SHORT ACCOUNT of the Behaviour of the Rebel ARMY, while at *Hamilton*, in a Letter to a Friend at *Edinburgh*.

WE have at last got a Visit from your formerly troublesome Neighbours, which we neither expected, desired nor wanted. ---- However, their Stay was but short; but at the same Time very troublesome.---- Upon *Tuesday* the 24th *December*, in the Afternoon, there came in here, 1900 Horse and Foot, tho' they gave themselves out for 2500. They were commanded (if I may call it so) by the Lords, *George Murray*, *Nairn*, *Elcho*, *Ogilvie*, and *Glenbucket* and others.---- Upon the *Wednesday* Morning, Part of them went off for *Glasgow*; and that Afternoon, their Prince, the Duke of *Perth*, their *French* Ambassador, *Lochyell*, and others, with Part of the *Clans*, came in. Both these Nights, the People of the Town, tho' greatly throng'd, were at greater Peace, than on the *Thursday's* Night, when the *Camerons*, *MacPhersons*, and *MacDonalds* of *Clan-Ronald's* Party came up; after having burnt some Houses in *Lismabague*, and rified one of the Minister's Houses; and had it not been for two of *Lochmoidart's* Brothers, they would have laid the whole Town in Ashes, and plundered the Country about) and then indeed we felt the Effects of an undisciplin'd ungovernable Army of *Highland* Robbers, who took no more Notice of their nominal Prince, or Commanders, than a Pack of ill-bred Hounds. The Provisions, Ale and Spirits, beginning to run short in the Town, they threatened the People with Death, or the burning their Houses, unless such Victuals and Drink were got as they call'd for; which Victuals were not of the coarse Sort, Herrings, Onions, and a Butter, and a Cheese,----which we look'd upon as their best Food, such they would not taste. The People of *England* have taught them such a bad Custom, that they would scarce taste good Salt-beef and Greens, the meanest of them calling for roast or fried fresh Victuals; if such were not got, they treated the People very ill. My Lodgers were so luxurious, that they would not taste boil'd Pork, a little pickled, unless we would cause dress it in a Frying-pan, with fresh Butter.---Amongst this Set of Ruffians there were some civil People, some of whom my Aunt, and her two Neighbours had the good Fortune to get for Lodgers. I had no less than 33 of them, the last Night, of the worst Kind, besides Horses and naked Whores.

Our Subscribers, Volunteers and Militia, were obliged to leave the Place; amongst whom were, your Good-Brother and myself, so I had not the Trouble of them; tho' their three Nights Lodging, with what they stole from me, cost me about 6 l. *Sterling*. They have rifled several Houses in this Neighbourhood, and broke and destroy'd what they could not carry off, particularly, Captain *Crawford's*, *Thomas Hatten's*, at *Smiddy-Croft* and *Woodside*.

The Prince went a hunting upon *Thursday*, in the Duke's Park; he shot two Pheasants, two Woodcocks, two Hares, and a young Buck, all which were carried in Triumph. He dined at Chatleroy, where I saw him, but could not find out this Angel-like Prince amongst the whole Rabble, till he was pointed out to me.---While here, they strip'd the People of their Shoes upon the Street, and took what they thought proper for them, refusing to be hinder'd by any of their Officers.

There was not any of this Rabble, but what were possess'd of Plenty of Gold, even the smallest Boys, and nakedest Whores. We were freed from these troublesome Neighbours upon *Friday* Morning the 27th; who left us nothing but an innumerable Multitude of Vermin, and their Excrements; which they left not only in our Bed-Chambers, but in our very Beds. The civilest Kind held their Doups over the Stock of the Beds, like Crows shiting over the Nest. Our Town smells of them yet, but the Peoples Spirits are getting up, for while they were here, they look'd like dead Corps. They stop'd us from a merry Christmass, but God be thanked, we were bless'd with a merry New-Year's Day. I wish you a happy New-Year, and Peace, which we now begin to learn to value. All Friends, being here assembled, join in good Wishes and Services to you. I am, &c.

Hamilton, 6th *January*, 1746.

N. B. That the Facts contain'd in the above Letter is attested to be true by some other Persons of undoubted Credit who live in *Hamilton*; and that besides burning a House in *Lismabague*, which contain'd five Families; they dragg'd a Woman up and down the Fields, who had lately brought forth a Child, until she fainted, and then some of them had as much Humanity as to cast Water on her Face, and so let her ly till she recovered. These polite *Highlanders*, who keep'd their Sheets clean, in the Manner mentioned in the above Letter, carried them off amongst their Spoils.

During the '45, private letters were frequently printed as a way of disseminating news — and propaganda. (National Library of Scotland, Blk.736)

upon Friday Morning the 27th; who left us nothing but an innumerable Multitude of Vermin, and their Excrements; which they left not only in our Bed-Chambers, but in our very Beds. The civilest Kind held their Doups over the Stock of the Beds, like Crows shiting over the Nest. Our Town smells of them yet.

This is part of a private letter published as propaganda but there is likely to be some truth in it. The artist William Hogarth depicted the Guards on their way to Finchley as a licentious rabble; and a series of robberies around Edinburgh in early 1745 was blamed on soldiers billeted in the area. Playing host to a large body of armed men — government or rebel — was not a pleasant experience in the mid-eighteenth century, when so many private soldiers and sailors were society's outcasts. Genuine volunteers rubbed shoulders with the retainers of landed officers and men driven to take up arms from dire want or in return for a small bounty, some of them fugitive debtors or wanted criminals. In wartime, unemployed men could be pressed into service by force. In Scotland the uprising in 1745–6 was the last occasion on which feudal superiors forced out unwilling vassals for service by burning their homes, but the experience of doing someone else's bidding without understanding why was familiar to soldiers on both sides, as can be judged from a squib which appeared in the *Caledonian Mercury* after the battle of Fontenoy:

> I often think of an honest Country Recruit, who was marching in order to embark when we made our first Exportation of Troops in 1742. By the Interest of a Mug of Beer I had the Opportunity of asking him some Questions, one of which was, For what was he going abroad? — *They tell me, Master, to fight; and egad I'll down with 'em an I can.* — But for whom do you fight, Friend? — *Nay, nay, that I can't tell: But 'tis for some d—n'd Queen or another: I suppose you know her Name, thof I don't.*

A china plate depicting Highland soldiers, manufactured after the rebellion as a souvenir. (The Pilgrim Press Ltd., Derby)

A waistcoat and trews believed to have belonged to Prince Charles. (By kind permission of the Trustees of the West Highland Museum, Fort William and The Pilgrim Press Ltd., Derby)

Whatever their reasons for enlisting, in an age when a musket fired 'three score yards' and armies closed on one another with stabbing weapons, soldiers were brutalised by their bloody trade and the harsh discipline needed to keep them in it; pay was irregular and looting commonly followed a battle. Among the comfortably-off there was such a dread of having troops quartered in a household that it was sometimes used as a means of punishment. This was the origin of much of the animosity in the south-west of Scotland towards Highlanders, as Highland troops had been used in this way by the government of Charles II in an effort to crush the Covenanting movement in the 1670s (the so-called 'Highland Host'). Although the Highlanders were in some respects superior to the king's infantry in the way they were motivated and disciplined by pressures from within their clan, brigandage was strong in their tradition, and this, together with their wild appearance and Gaelic speech, created the general impression that they were barbarians. As Lochiel found to his astonishment, when he had inquired why there were no children around in many of the English villages they passed through, Whig propagandists had had no trouble convincing country people that Highlanders were in the habit of eating infants.

Given the real hatred which existed between Presbyterians from the west and many Highlanders, it is perhaps not surprising that when the army marched to Glasgow for a review, Charles was recorded as saying that it was a fine town but he found he had no friends there. To underline the point there is a tradition that a pistol was snapped or even fired at him as he rode through the Saltmarket. In the week they spent in Glasgow the Jacobite commissariat industriously levied large quantities of clothes and shoes, as well as money fines, from the merchants of Glasgow and Paisley, to punish their forwardness in raising troops for King George. The prince set up his headquarters in the Trongate and seemed to recover his poise. He donned his finery, dined in state and even danced with Glasgow ladies at balls. He was heartened to find that there had been little desertion on the retreat, and further good news arrived. Lord Lewis Gordon, who had been recruiting and raising money in the north-east, had repulsed an attack by some independent companies of Lord Loudoun's command near Inverurie. Some 1200 men

Facies Civitatis GLASGOW ab Oriente Estevo. The Prospect of ỹ Town of GLASGOW from ỹ North East.
17.

under Gordon were now marching with Lord Drummond's force and a number of Frasers, Mackintoshes and Mackenzies, to link up with the army which had gathered at Perth. By the time the Jacobites left Glasgow on 3 January 1746 it looked as if Charles would shortly have more than 9000 men at his command.

The welcome reflection that he would soon outweigh government forces in Scotland for the first time was marred by a report brought to him by two officers who had escaped from Carlisle: after a short bombardment the besieged garrison had surrendered to the Duke of Cumberland on 30 December. The only concession extracted — being reserved to await the king's pleasure instead of being put to the sword — hardly redeemed the prince's misjudgment, particularly in the light of his earlier refusal to send captured prisoners to France as hostages. Previous mistakes could be blamed on the army council. Since Derby Charles had refused to call any councils: this setback was his own doing. It struck at him. Not long after the army left Glasgow for Stirling he fell ill with influenza and withdrew to the house of Sir Hugh Patterson at Bannockburn where he was nursed by his host's niece, Clementina Walkinshaw, who was to become his mistress.

*****

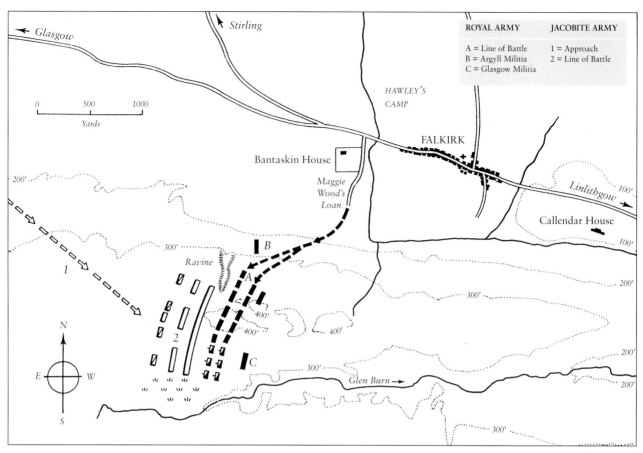

The battle of Falkirk, 17 January 1746.

After the fall of Carlisle, the Duke of Cumberland returned to London. The French still had troops ready to embark at Boulogne and Dunkirk, and Admiral Vernon had expressed fears that he might not be able to stop an invasion. The command in Scotland had been offered to Marshal Wade, who declined it. It was given instead to General Henry Hawley, who made his way to Edinburgh from Newcastle, arriving on 6 January with strong reinforcements. In the weeks after the Jacobites had evacuated the capital, Price's and Ligonier's foot and the reformed dragoons who had fled at Prestonpans had been joined by a militia regiment from the west and some local recruits. Detachments were sent to Stirling to guard the fords across the Forth, and their presence, added to a shortage of carts, had prevented Lord Strathallan carrying out the prince's order to reinforce him. These detachments were withdrawn when Charles's army appeared at Glasgow and the two Jacobite commands were able to link up near Stirling unimpeded. Unwilling to leave a government strongpoint on the Forth estuary, the Jacobites decided that Stirling Castle should be their next objective, and the town was attacked on the 5th and taken two days later. Stirling Castle was no more vulnerable to a besieging force without heavy artillery than Edinburgh Castle had been, but when the Jacobites received intelligence from the capital of the arrival of twelve infantry regiments and five squadrons of dragoons, they decided to lay siege to the castle in the hope of bringing Hawley onto their ground. The French engineer who supervised the operations, M.

Stirling Castle as it is today.
(Historic Scotland)

Mirabel de Gordon ('M. Admirable' as he came to be called), was an incompetent drunkard; since the prince lay ill, and Lord George Murray was reconnoitring in West Lothian, this initially passed unnoticed by senior officers. Murray visited the prince, but only to request bluntly that, as an emergency measure, he relinquish power to a handful of his colonels. Charles was scathing. A long letter refuting the general's arguments ended, 'I…shall only tell you that my authority may be taken from me by violence, but I shall never resign it like an idiot.' With a battle looming the quarrel was shelved, for the time being.

General Hawley's nickname among his own troops was 'Hangman'. This was said to derive from an order to display the skeleton of an executed soldier in the regimental guard room. Harsh and arrogant, vigour was his only quality. He had fought at Sheriffmuir in 1715 and believed that the Highlander was a contemptible enemy, who would flee from disciplined cavalry. He erected gibbets in the capital in anticipation of his forthcoming victory. Meanwhile, Major-General John Huske rode to Linlithgow with the vanguard on 13 January. When Lord Elcho reported a large body of troops moving westwards, the Jacobites retreated to Falkirk and then to Bannockburn. A force of 8500 Jacobites drew up for a battle on the 15th and 16th, but Hawley did not arrive at Falkirk until the 16th, where he was joined by over 1000 Argyllshire militia led by Campbell of Mamore's son, Lieutenant-Colonel John Campbell.

The two armies were similar in size, but the rebels were quartered over a wide area and so in danger from a sudden attack. There was a clamour for action. Knowing that the site of Hawley's camp was overlooked, Lord George Murray decided that it was possible to reach the high moorland above it by stealth. While some units staged a diversion on the Stirling road the bulk of the regiments hurried to Falkirk Muir by back roads. Hawley had no patrols out on the 17th and was fortunate that warnings reached him at Callendar House, where Lady Kilmarnock's designing hospitality and his own sense of security had kept him until mid-afternoon. Eventually, he stood his men to arms, but made no other move. Only late in the afternoon, when it was obvious that the Jacobites aimed at seizing the high ground, were Hawley's men ordered to move up the hill to dispute it. Perhaps crucially, the artillery stuck fast in a bog near the camp. Writing from Edinburgh, Lord Milton described what happened next in a letter to Duncan Forbes:

Andrew Fletcher, Lord Milton (1692-1766). As Lord Justice Clerk, Milton was one of the four principal law officers who carried on the day-to-day administration of government in Scotland during the rebellion. (In a Scottish private collection)

A Dreadfull Storm of rain and wind from the South, happened at this instant, in the teeth of our Army, as they mounted up the hill, bad Roads and uneaven Ground put our folks quite out of Breath, when the Armys drew nigh their right was covered by a Morass, and their left reached only to our Center. The Dragoons were ordered to begin the Charge and were well led on by their Officers, received the fire, then reeled and many of them fled, numbers of bye Standers running off with them, struck a pannick, and people at some Distance observing such a run, concluded all gone, and scattered terror even to this Town…so many of the Dragoons being fled, our left Wing exposed gave way, without being I may say attacked, at least most of them. The Rebells did not make use of this Advantage by following in pursuite. Two Regiments on the Right; Burrells commanded by Lt. Colonel Rich, and Legoniers foot, by Lieut. Colonel Stanhope, both under command of Brigadier Cholmondeley made a noble stand, firing in platoons, and saving the fire of the front Rank, whereby they kept the Rebells at a distance, advanced on them and fired till the Rebells thought proper to run off, up the Hill as fast as they came down. General Huske had during this time rallied a great body of Foot behind these Regiments, as Brigadier Mordent did the Remainder of the Foot near Falkirk.

Milton's eye-witnesses misled him somewhat. They neglected to tell him that a large enough contingent of the clans had stayed together to chase them to Falkirk. The impression of casualties they gave him, 'Our loss is not computed above 200, the Rebells thrice that number, our greatest Loss is Reputation', aimed at concealing Hawley's embarrassment. At a cost to themselves of some thirty to fifty men killed and about eighty wounded, the Jacobites had scattered part of his command, killing as many as 400 and taking over 300 prisoners. The remainder, after an unsuccessful attempt to burn their camp at Falkirk, retreated first to Linlithgow and then to Edinburgh, leaving most of the artillery and large amounts of stores and ammunition to be taken. Among the 464 men Hawley later admitted losing was Colonel Sir Robert Munro, commander of the Black Watch at Fontenoy, the senior officer among 23 killed. His official report was as vague as it could be with regard to the wounded and missing, and made no mention of casualties among the Glasgow militia, shattered by the Highlanders' charge.

Milton had not yet heard how, the next day, the stripped corpses of the government soldiers resembled a ghastly flock of sheep on the wet hillside (a sight still recalled in Falkirk in the nineteenth century). However, the complacency in his letter — written four days after the event — is a comment on the Jacobites' inability to exploit their victory. In a battle begun with haste, approaching dusk, and in driving rain and sleet, both armies had splintered and dispersed in several directions, confused and seeking shelter. The wet weather continuing the following day had prevented an immediate pursuit: Hawley got safely to Edinburgh. The destruction of the government's army there might have restored the Stuarts to the throne of Scotland, but with several thousand trained men to defend it, it would be more difficult to capture the capital a second time. The prince lacked the means of moving artillery rapidly for a siege. He hesitated before eventually taking what many thought was a fatal decision. Burdened with a heavy cold, he was persuaded by his acolytes to continue the siege of Stirling Castle, while he returned to Bannockburn House. Foreseeably, numbers of clansmen took advantage of the lull in activity and returned home with their booty. The Chevalier Johnstone was one of the many officers left chafing with frustration. The bitterness stayed with him:

The absurd wish to possess an insignificant castle which could be of no real utility to us produced a series of effects which ruined the Prince's enterprise and brought a great number of his partisans to the scaffold.

The truth was that neither side was happy with the outcome of the battle of Falkirk. While Hawley vented his rage with a string of hangings, shootings and dismissals to punish cowardice and desertion, the atmosphere at Falkirk was poisoned with recriminations. Anger at Hawley's escape fed on shortcomings which came to light in the battle. Most of the officers and men had behaved as well as they were ever likely to in an engagement; but a few experienced officers had always expressed doubts as to whether undisciplined men like the Highlanders could execute a battle-plan if they were exposed to sustained fire from small-arms or artillery. The battle seemed to have made their point: shoot-and-rush had not been enough. From a bad position the clansmen's advance on the enemy's right had been hampered by a gully. Taking advantage of this, a spur of infantry regiments had poured a steady fire on the Scots, not only checking them but driving them back with losses. In addition, the way their counterparts handled their men to achieve an orderly retreat made an impression on the Jacobite officers. Whether charging forward or being pushed back, their own men were often out of control. This observation did not augur well for the future. As Lord George Murray noted:

> The best of the Highland officers…were absolutely convinced that except they could attack the enemy at very considerable advantage, either by surprise or by some strong situation of ground, or a narrow pass, they could not expect any great success, especially if their numbers were no ways equal, and that a body of regular troops was absolutely necessary to support them, when they should at any time go in, sword in hand.

The prince was not disconcerted. As far as he was concerned two battles had been fought and both had been won. Once again his army was invincible, sweeping aside his father's enemies. Such confidence might have spread if the next step had been either bold or successful, but the siege of Stirling Castle merely exposed the failings of the Jacobites in another unfamiliar aspect of regular warfare. Stirling's veteran commander, Major-General Blakeney, was an intelligent and experienced soldier who appreciated that time was on the government's side. He withheld his superior firepower during the weeks that the besiegers took to construct a ramshackle battery. When it was completed he opened fire and demolished it, killing many of the French and Lowland troops involved. This abrupt failure was disheartening. It came on top of bad feeling among the Macdonalds, following the accidental shooting of Angus Og, commander of the Glengarry regiment, by a Clanranald Macdonald, at Falkirk. The number of desertions seemed to be increasing daily. When it was heard that the Duke of Cumberland was expected shortly in Edinburgh with three more regiments, a mood of despondency began to spread through the various Jacobite camps at the prospect of another battle.

William Blakeney (1672-1761). An Irishman, he first saw service as an ensign in 1695, and had spent much of his long career as a junior officer. He was promoted major-general and lieutenant-governor of Stirling Castle in 1744. (National Library of Scotland; on loan to the Scottish National Portrait Gallery)

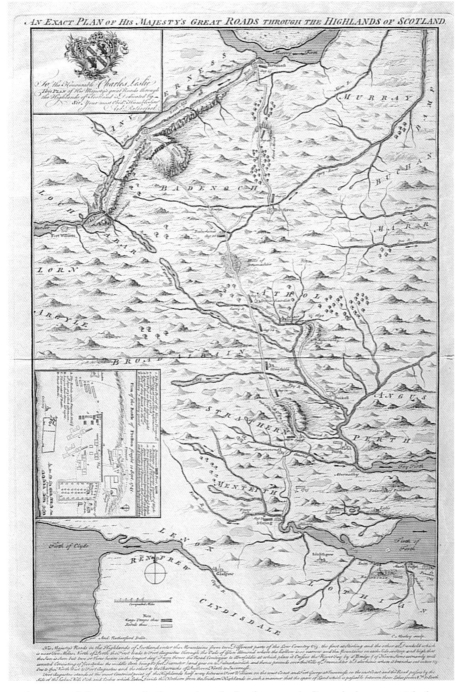

Map published prior to the battle of Falkirk, showing the campaign in Scotland in 1745. (National Library of Scotland, EMS.s.90b)

A powerful group of clan colonels had never believed that, unaided, an army drawn from northern Scotland could overthrow the constitution of the United Kingdom. After Derby they could only be rallied to the prince's standard by appeals to their valour and ancient habits of loyalty and deference. Despite what their hearts said, their heads told them that if the campaign was to be ended by a hammer blow, it was more likely to come from the British army, and the battle of Falkirk emphasised this. They could not say so: their tradition allowed no place for fear; but nor were clan chiefs in the habit of asking their people to sacrifice themselves when there was nothing to be gained. This placed them in a dilemma between loyalty and resentment, which they hid with increasing difficulty. The prince, on the other hand, appeared unconcerned at having difficulties concealed behind false pretences: it was his preferred method of dealing with them. His crazed optimism was the foundation of the collective self-deceit which underpinned the rebellion. Unfortunately, morale woven from such rotten thread was never likely to survive the first signs that the government was gaining the upper hand. General Blakeney provided the signs.

Without a forum to carry the issue by a vote, on 29 January an exhausted lieutenant-general and seven demoralised colonels signed their names to a memorandum which advocated a retreat to the Highlands. It passed for advice to the prince; in fact, it was a mutiny in all but name. 'Good God! Have I lived to see this', was the prince's reaction when, on the 30th, he read the names of Lochiel, Keppoch, Clanranald, Ardshiel, Lochgarry, Scothouse and the Master of Lovat beside that of Lord George — all advising that the army was in no condition to fight if the enemy suddenly advanced. Charles struck his head repeatedly on the wall in disbelief. To him a retreat to the mountains made no sense other than as a last refuge. Scotland would be lost to the Stuarts as England and Wales had been. Lord George was simply misguided in thinking that the Jacobites could triumph in a drawn-out conflict: no large body of men could support themselves in the Highlands in winter. At this point the prince must have felt like Shakespeare's Macbeth:

> ...I am in blood
> Stepp'd in so far, that, should I wade no more,
> Returning were as tedious as go o'er. *(Act III, Scene IV)*

He had nothing but scorn for the hope he scented among the chiefs that they could somehow escape the consequences of their act of revolt if only they could return to their glens. His officers had been the principal agents in a bloody and terrifying upheaval. The fact that when they rose in arms they were serving the colours of a man (to the Whigs, a usurper) in whom they had little personal faith would count for nothing when their lives and fortunes were being weighed by the victorious Hanoverians. The prince sent Sir Thomas Sheridan to Falkirk to plead the futility of such hopes. 'Can we imagin,' Charles wrote to them on the 30th 'that where we go the Ennemy will not follow, and at last oblige us to a Battel which we now decline...' When they would not change their minds he gave orders for a retreat to begin: 'if you are all resolved upon it I must yield; but I take God to witness that it is with the greatest reluctance, and that I wash my hands of the fatal consequences wch I foresee but cannot help'.

*****

On 2 February the prince held a review at Crieff. He was angered to find that the number of desertions had been exaggerated. But Lord George Murray brought fury of his own to the first council meeting held since 5 December. He had planned an orderly retreat from Stirling. Instead, he found himself a helpless spectator at a débâcle. When the regiments caught the spirit of mutiny they streamed north in disorder: one detachment was cut off in Stirling and captured; equipment was abandoned (including the clothes which had been requisitioned at Glasgow); and the army's magazine exploded, destroying St Ninians' church and killing bystanders. When Murray came across O'Sullivan on the road there was a heated argument in front of the troops and the lieutenant-general had to be restrained after swearing at the Irishman. At Crieff he demanded to know who had countermanded his orders, 'for', he declared, 'it was worth the Government at London's while to give a hundred thousand pounds to any who would have given such an advice & got it follow'd'. The prince would not be drawn. Riding to the devil, he was not interested in Lord George's complaints about the horse. With difficulty, the council decided to split the army into three. The prince would lead the Highland regiments north by the main road; Lord Ogilvy's and the Farquharsons would go by Coupar Angus to Speyside; and Lord George would take the Lowland regiments and the cavalry to Montrose and Aberdeen. They would rendezvous at Inverness, which was presently held for the government by Lord Loudoun.

Of the two Campbells commanding the militia in Scotland, Lord Loudoun had a more difficult task than his namesake, Major-General John Campbell of Mamore, who was attempting to secure the Duke of Argyll's fief from Inverary Castle. Although older and not in good health, General Campbell could count on the loyalty of his men; most of the problems he faced in garrisoning Fort William and a chain of smaller strongholds on the Argyllshire coast were logistical. But as they were from the north west and the Isles, some of Loudoun's militia companies were unreliable. Many men in them would more willingly have worn the prince's colours. They were harnessed for the government by the skill of Lord President Duncan Forbes in manipulating the ambitions and fears of their chiefs. (One of these, Macleod of Macleod, was said to have brought some of his men from Skye to Inverness by the ruse of supplying them with white cockades, just as if Charlie was *his* darling.) Forbes knew that even if the militia was not an effective fighting force, he was at least denying men to the pretender. As events proved, and as Lord George had predicted, the king's generals would not risk penetrating into the mountains until the Jacobites were a spent force, so the militia was deployed to hamper the prince. Although they met with little success in their encounters and made a poor impression on the Captain-General, the Duke of Cumberland, the effort the rebels expended on them throughout February and March 1746 was grist to his mill.

The Duke of Cumberland had been appointed to command in Scotland on 25 January and left London immediately. He arrived in Scotland, as he would depart six months or so later, trailing smoke and ashes. Following the earlier example of the Lancashire towns, a mob at Newcastle greeted his arrival by

Duart and Tioram castles in Argyllshire, from Board of Ordnance maps prepared for use by government forces. (National Library of Scotland, Z3/28d)

John Campbell, 4th Earl of Loudoun (1705-1782), by Allan Ramsay. (Scottish National Portrait Gallery)

Prospectus Regis Palatis LIMNUCHENSIS. *The Prospect of Their Maj.ties Palace of* LINLITHGOW.

10.

The former palace of the Stuarts at Linlithgow went up in flames when the fires lit by government troops quartered there got out of control. From Slezer's Theatrum Scotiae. *(National Library of Scotland)*

(the newspapers reported) burning a large house 'where a Popish Chapel was kept…[T]he House and Appurtenances being vastly large, it was a terrible Sight, and was very near the Height of the Blaze when the Duke pass'd by, which he did almost close to it, being the main Street in the Town'. He reached Edinburgh on the 30th. Although he was in time to spare a few soldiers from Hawley's rancour, on the same day that St Ninians was shaken by the prince's powder, the old palace at Linlithgow was left to burn after being accidentally set on fire by government troops.

Cumberland marched to Perth, arriving on 6 February. By the time General Campbell joined his son there with reinforcements of militia (bringing the total with the army to over 1000 again) it was to discover that the duke had already sanctioned the burning of Sir Henry Stirling of Ardoch's house, along with some others, so that his men 'might have some sweets with all their fatigues'. On 7 February Sir Andrew Agnew, the lieutenant-colonel of Mamore's regiment, the Scots Fusiliers, was sent to seize Blair Castle which the prince had evacuated. On the 13th he was ordered to ravage Atholl. When Cumberland sent General Campbell back to the west coast in mid-February he was to relay orders to the navy to lay waste to disloyal 'countries'. Unfortunately, one of these 'countries' belonged to the Duke of Argyll, and some of the rebels were his tenants.

On 10 February the prince's army captured Ruthven barracks, which had defied them the previous summer. Moving to Inverness, on 16 February the prince stopped at Moy Hall, residence of Lady ('Colonel') Anne Macintosh. Somehow Lord Loudoun got wind of Charles being nearby with only a small force and set out with 1500 men to capture him. He confidently expected to be £30,000 richer before the night was out. Lady Macintosh was warned, however, and her blacksmith went with a handful of men to try to hold Loudoun off while the prince escaped. By firing off a few balls and calling out to each other they convinced the militia that they were about to confront a large force. When their piper was killed, Loudoun's men panicked and hurried back to Inverness Castle. The prince capitalised on the 'Rout of Moy' to assault Inverness. At his approach Loudoun retreated across the Moray Firth, taking all the available boats with him. The prince took the town and shortly afterwards the castle (the original Fort George) with its much needed stores.

Although the fall of Inverness was an unhappy blow for the Whigs, Cumberland was not inclined to drive north in a hurry. While the Jacobites were repelling surprise attacks and storming fortresses, government forces were employed in burning farms and homes. To the Whigs the rebellion had at first been merely an obstruction to British foreign policy; their attitude changed abruptly when it came within a few days' march of ousting the ruling Guelph family, and those in their interest, from power. Reprisals motivated by fear are often vicious, and since the flames of religious hatred

Ruthven barracks, Kingussie.
(Historic Scotland)

required little fanning, the Duke of Cumberland had found it useful to whip up anti-Jacobite and anti-Catholic feeling to hinder the rebels' retreat in England. But Cumberland was not alone in being determined that the leniency which had followed previous insurrections in Scotland should not be repeated. The Highlands were seeing the first stage of an official policy whose aim was, in the words of Cumberland's secretary, Sir Everard Fawkener, to 'bruise those bad seeds spread about this country so as they may never shoot again'.

7 CULLODEN

It was surely wrong to set up the Royal Standard without having positive assurance from his most Christian Majesty [Louis XV] that he would assist you with all his might.
(LORD GEORGE MURRAY TO PRINCE CHARLES EDWARD, 17 APRIL 1746)

ON 8 February 1746, King George's son-in-law, Prince Frederick of Hesse-Cassel, arrived at Leith with 6000 Hessians to replace the Dutch troops which had had to be withdrawn when Lord John Drummond arrived from France. The Duke of Cumberland returned to Edinburgh briefly in mid-February for consultations, and it was at a meeting at Lord Milton's house that the Lord Justice Clerk persuaded the commander that the prince's army would not simply melt away, as some officers — with an eye on the deteriorating situation in the Austrian Netherlands — hoped it might. The duke prepared for a campaign in which every screw would have to be turned. Unlike his adversary, however, he was in a position to make arrangements for provisions and money to follow his army and took full advantage of the willingness of loyalists in Scotland and the north of England to pay their taxes before they were even due.

The Highland Chace, or the Pursuit of the Rebels. *(National Library of Scotland; on loan to the Scottish National Portrait Gallery)*

Even as he made use of his brother-in-law to prevent the rebels from returning to the Lowlands through Perthshire, and Milton to organise the civil authorities, Cumberland decided that they were men of the wrong kidney for the task of punishing rebellion. The chivalry of one and the legal scruples of the other reminded him uncomfortably that many men of high rank in Scotland who claimed to support his family had roots in the same soil which was the seed-bed of rebellion. He complained to London about a climate of sympathy for the rebels which had its origin in the outworn quasi-feudal principles which many 'loyal' Scots shared with them. The rebellion provided abundant grounds for suspicion. Lord George Murray, after all, had once kissed the king's hand in return for a pardon, and Ewan Macpherson was one of a number who had laid aside the king's commission to join the rebels; there were grandees at court, and even officers under him, who had fathers or brothers in the rebel army. By the time Cumberland had gauged the reaction of ordinary people on his march up the coast to Aberdeen in Murray's footsteps, his view was that 'nothing will cure this but some stroke of military authority and severity'. The only kind of loyalty which would have its reward was the fanatical kind.

As the most influential of the Scottish peers, the Duke of Argyll was theoretically in a position to act as a counterweight to this prejudice. By early in the new year, however, with the Jacobite army now out of England and a French invasion looking less likely by the day, a shake-up occurred at Westminster. The Pelhamites had recruited support for their long-running battle against the king's interference in policy-making from a group led by William Pitt, which was keen to chastise Scottish Whigs for their complacency in the early stages of the rising. As a result, the ineffectual Secretary of State for Scotland, the Marquis of Tweeddale, resigned his office in January 1746. The administration finally won its battle, forcing George II to accept its terms, by resigning *en masse* on 11 February, thereby causing a short-lived (48 hour) crisis. The cabinet was never likely to endorse the Earl of Chesterfield's proposal to starve the whole of Scotland into submission, and Argyll was not in serious political danger himself. Nevertheless, some of the ground was cut from under the feet of his protégés in Scotland, who included the senior law officers. Consequently, the Duke of Cumberland's desire to set up a temporary military government more or less outside the rule of law became that much easier to fulfil.

Provost Ross's house acted as home to part of Battereau's regiment of foot, when the Duke of Cumberland's forces arrived in Aberdeen on 25 February 1746. Shortly afterwards, a grand ball was held in Marischal College in honour of the duke. (National Trust for Scotland)

❊❊❊❊❊

After an arduous journey up the coast in awful weather, Lord George Murray joined the prince at Inverness just before the fall of Fort George. He left a force at Aberdeen and another was posted to dispute the passage of the River Spey. It was hoped support would arrive from France before government forces closed the coastal ports. Some did: men picked from Berwick's and Fitzjames's regiments arrived on 21 and 22 February (with a subsidy of around £1200), but not enough. Even allowing for the 359 men who were on board two captured transports, too little help came from the Continent. The responsibility for this lay with Jacobite emissaries who were in the habit of deceiving foreign ministers about affairs in Britain, preferring instead to romance powerful men for their own ends. It may have disgusted the Earl Marischal, but the lean years in exile had made selling themselves and puffing their projects to patrons second nature to many Jacobite conspirators. When Cumberland's vanguard seized Aberdeen on 25 February it did not cut off a large French relieving force, since no such force existed: in the hope of gaining advancement through bearing good news, the officers sent to France had represented it to the king as not necessary. It was what His Most Christian Majesty wanted to hear.

With the Royal Navy in command of the Moray Firth, and Lord Loudoun's militia in possession of a fleet of inshore boats, it was possible that his force might link up with Cumberland's and seize the Spey crossing. A Jacobite force was despatched to Ross-shire in pursuit and then, when the militia crossed the Dornoch Firth, to Sutherland. The great cuts in the land that are the Moray, Cromarty and Dornoch firths made approach difficult since the militia commander had the only sea transport. When a force large enough to confront Loudoun reached the head of a firth, he had the option of retreating north overland or taking sail south again. The situation baffled the local Jacobite commander, Lord Cromarty, so Lord George Murray was sent into Ross-shire. His assessment was that nothing could be done unless boats could be brought from further afield, and the Jacobites fell back on Dingwall while vessels were collected. A flotilla was assembled at Findhorn, but the crews had to await a thick fog in mid-March before they could be moved to Tain to embark any clansmen.

The Duke of Perth was once again acting as a lieutenant-general and it was he who commanded the invasion of Sutherland. A surprise landing near Dornoch captured 200 of Loudoun's men but, in permitting them time to negotiate their surrender, Perth and O'Sullivan gave Loudoun and Forbes the chance to flee with the bulk of the militia. The two Whig leaders eventually reached Skye, while enough of their men remained in Sutherland to thwart the Jacobites' attempts to overawe it and bring out the few small clans in Caithness and Orkney which were sympathetic. The combined success and failure of this operation established a pattern which was repeated throughout March. The Jacobites were to be continually reminded of the besetting disappointment of the uprising: nowhere were they recognised as the civil power in the absence of drawn swords.

The hub of the revolt was now at Inverness; yet with the Hanoverian authorities in a position to weaken the spokes near the rim in several places, clan chiefs felt the pull of suffering inflicted on their own 'countries'. Several regiments were allowed to go their separate ways, partly because this eased the problem of supplying the men as provisions dwindled. Fort William had long been a thorn to Camerons and Macdonalds in Lochaber and, after blowing up Fort Augustus with a fortunate shot on 5 March, Lochiel, Keppoch and Brigadier Stapleton marched to besiege it. Similarly, Lord

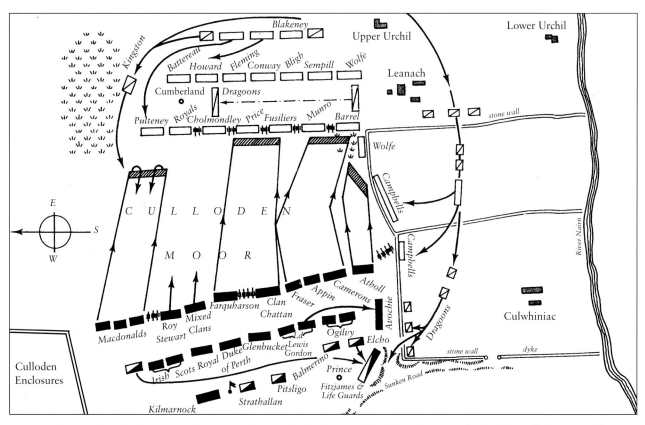

Upper Urchil
Lower Urchil
Leanach
Blakeney
Kingston
Batterau
Howard Fleming Conway Bligh Sempill Wolfe
Cumberland Dragoons
stone wall
Pulteney Royals Cholmondley Price Fusiliers Munro Barrel
Wolfe
Campbells
C U L L O D E N
Campbells
M O O R
Dragoons
Culwhiniac
Atholl
Camerons
Appin
Fraser
Farquharson Clan
Chattan
Avochie
Roy Mixed
Stewart Clans
Macdonalds
Lewis Ogilvy
Glenbucket Gordon Elcho
Irish Scots Royal Duke
of Perth
stone wall dyke
Balmerino Prince
Pitsligo Fitzjames &
Strathallan Life Guards Sunken Road
Kilmarnock

River Nairn

Culloden
Enclosures

The battle of Culloden, 16 April 1746. (See also map on page 124)

George Murray linked up with Macpherson in Badenoch in an effort to dislodge government forces from Atholl. In a manoeuvre to rival the capture of Edinburgh, their joint forces seized thirty strongpoints in the early hours of 17 March, while the chiefs and just a handful of men hoodwinked Sir Andrew Agnew's regulars back into Blair Castle, where they too were besieged. On the 20th, the man who had largely been responsible for the capture of the *Hazard* sloop (which the prince had renamed after himself and sent to France for supplies), Major Nicholas Glascoe, led a successful attack against a garrison at Keith made up of Argyllshire militia and irregular cavalry.

By doing what they did best, moving quickly and attacking fiercely, the Highlanders rapidly amassed prisoners and seized territory — only for their efforts to appear pointless when their sieges ran up against the familiar obstacle of poor artillery incompetently manned (their one success, an engineer named Grant, was killed by a stray ball at Fort William). It was not clear who was harrassing whom when the rebels were forced to divide to deal with threats to their homes and kin while the government commander built up his forces virtually unmolested along the east coast, his supplies arriving safely by sea.

Maxwell of Kirkconnell noticed how, in theory, Charles was at the hub, directing operations: 'the Prince will appear greater about this time at Inverness, than either at Gladsmuir or at Falkirk'. In reality there was no centre for a period of time in February and March. Lord George arrived in Inverness, in the third week of February, to find that the prince had succumbed to pneumonia. After a short respite Charles was stricken with scarlet fever at Elgin (a 'spotted favour', O'Sullivan called it), which was the most serious of the illnesses he suffered from during the only winter he spent in Scotland. When Charles was ready to return to Inverness to take charge on 21 March he was forced to leave behind John Murray of Broughton, who fell ill in turn. The prince never again saw his secretary and the army lost the manager who, as even his hated namesake Lord George admitted, 'had always been extremely active in whatsoever regarded the providing for the army'. The secretary's replacement, his brother-in-law, John Hay of Restalrig, was to match 'M. Admirable' in incompetence.

More prisoners meant extra mouths to feed. Maxwell resumes:

> But this is the last favourable prospect we shall have of the Prince's affairs...[S]everal things contributed to this change, but nothing so much as the want of money, the principal sinew of war...The scarcity of money was concealed as long as possible; but when the common men were reduced to a weekly allowance of oatmeal, instead of their pay, which had formerly been very punctual, this sudden change was at first attended with discontent, murmurings, neglect of duty, and dismal apprehensions.

O'Sullivan concurred:

> Mony, Mony, was the word, there was none to give them. The Frinch Ambassedor kept bucle & tounge together & sustained the regular troops so-so, but the Prince had hardly where withall to pay the officers...the scarcenesse of mony made a great many grumble, & discouraged furiously every body.

Jacobites need only have read the press to know that parliament was in a position to sanction spending to rival the fabled east. As well as large subsidies to its allies in the War of the Austrian Succession, the government was voted £1,298,100 for the year 1746 to pay for 49,229 troops of the line, 11,550 marines and 40,000 seamen. Since the Jacobites were marching into England when the vote was taken, in November 1745, additional sums were granted to pay volunteers and militia. Not all the government commanders would have agreed, especially those in Scotland, but it certainly appeared as if the Treasury could come up with money whenever it was needed. The £15,000 or so which was on its way from France aboard the *Prince Charles* at the end of March was a pittance compared to the £100,000 or more which had purchased the services of Prince Frederick's Hessians — an army slightly larger than Charles's was to be at Culloden — and was even considerably less than the £26,000 which the *Caledonian Mercury* reported had been collected by the first week of April 1746, for Cumberland's use, in the county of Yorkshire alone. When it was heard that the *Prince Charles* had been chased into the Pentland Firth, and the treasure and 156 men seized by retainers of the Whig, Lord Reay, after the ship ran aground at Melness, the prince was forced to take the risk of sending Lord Cromarty with a large body of troops into the wilderness of north Sutherland in search of it.

'Samuel Macpherson in Highland uniform shot for desertion in the year 1743'. Two years before the rebellion a mutiny had occurred in the 43rd or Highland regiment (the Black Watch). During the crisis in 1745-46 the government recalled it from Flanders, but kept it in England. (National Library of Scotland; on loan to the Scottish National Portrait Gallery)

A receipt given to William Rose, the Lord President's grieve, for goods taken by the rebels from Culloden House, dated (perhaps spuriously) 16 April 1746. (National Library of Scotland, MS.2969, f.64)

Culloden Moor (National Trust for Scotland)

At the end of winter, when the royal army and navy had begun the process of creating shortages by burning or removing everything edible in rebel country, sixpence a day per man might not have bought much time for Charles, but it was the Jacobites' last lifeline. Money may not equal might, but the absence of it is usually quickly decisive in war.

Most Jacobites managed to draw some comfort from the fact that government forces came off worst in the exchanges which took place during February and March 1746. Others had portents of the cost of failure. The savagery of the sea-borne attack on the inhabitants of Morvern on 10 March, when, as reported to General Campbell, 'near 400 houses amongst which were several barns well fill'd with corn, horse, cows, meal and other provisions were distroy'd by fire and fire-arms', stunned Lochiel and Keppoch, so it was perhaps a blessing to the Jacobites that they were not privy to their opponent's plans in the event of the rebellion being crushed. The few humane Whigs who were received a shock on reading Cumberland's instructions. Campbell of Stonefield, the sheriff-depute of Argyll, wrote to the Duke of Argyll in London:

> The inevitable consequence of the execution of this order, is that the tender innocent babes must suffer with the guilty and that it will most probably introduce a horrible scene of murder, blood and rapin, not only in the rebels' country, but likeways into all those countrys that unluckily happen to be in their neighbourhood.

At least one loyalist's heart must have been wrung when news reached him of the battle which settled the issue.

* * * * *

In besieging Fort William and Blair Castle the Jacobites were attempting to reduce two very strong forts, without being in a position to cut off relief to either. Although Fort William was surrounded by hostile territory, men and supplies reached it via Loch Linnhe and rebel efforts to seal the loch at the Corran narrows failed. Once more their bombardment suffered from being directed by Mirabel. At Blair, Lord George was faced with trying to pierce walls seven feet thick with two light cannon. (To Sir Andrew Agnew the man was simply mad for trying to knock down his brother's house.) In keeping the 500 fusiliers inside from despoiling Atholl, Murray must have thought he was pursuing successfully the strategy which he had recommended to the prince after Falkirk. His belief that occupation of the Highlands made it possible to strike a bargain with the government is shown by the feelers he put out to the Prince of Hesse, the one man in the Hanoverian interest whom Murray thought he could trust. While Frederick did not have the power to arrange a cartel for prisoners against Cumberland's wishes, he did have more than enough men to march from Dunkeld to the relief of Blair Castle. Just before he arrived, with Lord Crawford, on 2 April, the garrison at Fort William saved itself by mounting a surprise attack on the Jacobite battery. A force under the command of Captain Carolina Scott captured or nailed up several cannon, making a further siege futile; within days the Jacobites had lost control over Atholl and Lochaber. Frederick was once again free to repudiate his brother-in-law's brutality, while men like Scott emulated it.

By the time Lord George returned to Inverness from Atholl, the Jacobites were less formidable. Charles headed a scattered and increasingly harried and ill-fed army, 'yt I cannot command any further than the chief Officers please' — but there was no repeat of the brown study of mid-December 1745, or his outburst at Bannockburn House. In public he reacted to the stranglehold his foe appeared to be gaining with a show of unconcern: he hunted by day and was resplendent at entertainments in the evening. As intended, the newspapers marvelled at such *sang-froid* when they expected to hear of a sickly wretch torturing himself with regrets at failure. But among the Jacobites there was criticism. Now that their pay consisted of a ration of meal, the rank and file were bewildered by a display of ease and ostentation. The officers, too, were left to ponder the prince's enduring preoccupation with ceremony and prerogative. Some of them took heart from it. Others considered that it showed that Charles was too insecure to cope with the practical business of commanding troops for very long. Had it become widely known, his reaction to the news that Lord George had treated with the Prince of Hesse would have lent weight to the latter view. There was no evidence that Lord George intended to betray his master, but a whispering campaign against him among Charles's cronies was so successful, that the prince obtained a promise from some Irish officers to watch the general, and to cut him down at the first sign of treachery in battle.

It is a measure of how much the initiative had slipped away from the rebels since the turn of the year that the government forces were now in a position to spring a surprise. When the level of the River Spey dropped, the Duke of Cumberland left Aberdeen for Cullen on 8 April, weeks, if not months, before his opponents expected him to stir. Lord George Murray had been wrong-footed. The prince on the other hand felt vindicated. The links which bound the Jacobite army to him had been getting more and more frail, but with Cumberland on the move, and the drip, drip, drip of aid from France cut off (news had finally arrived that, owing to ship losses, invasion plans had been cancelled), there was now a strong likelihood of a decisive conflict. The fact that not far from Culloden House there stood a stone which marked the defeat of Norwegian invaders by one of the early Scottish kings held the same naïve appeal for him which had prompted a call for a battle at Bannockburn when the Highland chiefs were against it. No time was lost sending orders to the commanders in various parts of the country to reassemble.

The rebels' last few days together as a force were a disastrous muddle. It was a boost to the British army that the Jacobites did not defend the crossing of the River Spey when they approached it on 12 April. It was the natural place for a stand, and Cumberland had expected Perth and Drummond to attempt an ambush, but they considered their force understrength for such an operation. When he met no opposition he was able to reach Elgin on 13 April, and Nairn the following day. Keppoch, Macpherson, Fraser and the detachment in Sutherland were still missing when all available men were drawn up on Drummossie Moor near Culloden to meet an expected attack on the 15th. But, as in similar circumstances at Bannockburn in January, none came. It was the duke's birthday, and a day's rest for his troops was capped by a celebration, with 'Billy' providing an issue of rum out of his own pocket. By early evening the Jacobite commanders were unanimously agreed that the opportunity existed to mount a surprise attack on a drunken camp. Prince Charles was not the only one who remembered events at Falkirk. In making this decision, however, they chose to overlook the fact that many of their men had spent several days without shelter and virtually without food, except for a single biscuit that day. The Jacobite army of September 1745 could have marched ten to twelve miles across rough terrain to attack a sleeping enemy before dawn. The army of April 1746 could not. When the attack had to be called off because not enough men had arrived in time to begin it, the prince could no more will all of his tired and hungry men back to Drummossie than his officers could drive some few starvelings forward to Nairn. The amount of men who, in the early hours of the morning, fell by the wayside to sleep or hurried to Inverness in a desperate search for food deprived the Jacobite army of perhaps four to five regiments at the battle of Culloden (British infantry regiments usually contained over 400 rank and file soldiers). The question is, which is more surprising: that a great many of the

Lord George Murray's orders to the Jacobite army, 14-15 April 1746. There is no mention of withholding quarter from the enemy but, as the historian W. Speck has pointed out, for the night attack on the British camp at Nairn to succeed, the much smaller Jacobite force would have needed to inflict large numbers of casualties in a short space of time. (The Royal Archives© Her Majesty Queen Elizabeth II)

men who returned fought with ferocity that day? Or that battle was joined when so many men were missing, and others unable to stand?

On the morning of 16 April everything was too late for the Jacobites. Although the Keppoch Macdonalds had returned, and some Frasers appeared early in the day, it was too late for Macpherson to arrive (he was a stiff march away); it was too late for Lords Cromarty and Macleod (they had been captured the day before and were being held at Dunrobin Castle); it was too late to sleep (nearly everyone tried to, but enemy patrols were sighted early and the army was called to arms); and it was too late to issue rations (there were no carts at Inverness to bring what food was available). The opportunity had passed to select a battlefield which did not play into the hands of the enemy's cavalry and artillery, despite Lord George's plea that 'there never could be more improper ground for Highlanders' than that chosen by the adjutant-general, O'Sullivan. The prince vetoed a move to a more suitable site beyond the River Nairn, because he feared that Cumberland might bypass them and seize Inverness. Sir Robert Strange, the prince's engraver and printer, is often quoted:

> What…can justify the deliberate folly and madness of fighting under such circumstances? But our time was come. We were at variance within ourselves: Irish intriguers and French politics were too predominant in our councils.

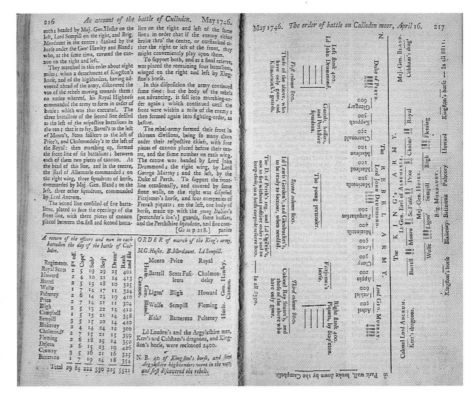

A report of the battle of Culloden in the Scots Magazine *of May 1746. (National Library of Scotland)*

(The Marquis d'Eguilles had in fact already begged Charles for a retreat and a delay and been refused.) The story has been preserved that the Highland chiefs had only been goaded to draw their men up on the moor by a remark that morning by Brigadier Walter Stapleton that the Scots were good troops until a crisis came. The dispositions made were hardly worth the name, and bear no comparison with those of the advancing British army. Any planning which existed related to a battle meant to be fought the day before, on a site some way to the east, and due to fatigue things were largely left to happen as they might. No one strove harder than the prince to inspire his troops with the will to fight as he rode along the lines, testing sword edges and making encouraging jests. However, without appreciating its full significance, he had earlier settled a dispute over the order of battle by relegating the Macdonalds to the left wing, when tradition gave them the right, and rendered them mutinous by doing so. When the Atholl brigade marched to the position the Macdonalds coveted, Lord George realised that the walled enclosures which they abutted gave cover to an outflanking force. Only a few horsemen could be spared to stand guard along them.

It may have occurred to the fighting men as they peered through the intermittent rain and hail that never before had they waited for the enemy to come to them, let alone withstood an artillery barrage. According to James Maxwell, when the lines of red coats hove into view late in the morning, 'they made a very good appearance; they were drawn up in three lines, or two lines and a large corps de reserve, with their cavalry on the wings. They had sixteen pieces of cannon placed in the intervals of the battalions of the first and second line.' A French officer, asked his opinion by the prince, answered

candidly for a superstitious army. He feared the day was already lost, he said, 'for he had never seen men advance to the attack in so cool and regular a manner as did their enemies'.

*****

The Duke of Cumberland is reported to have told his troops, 'Depend, depend my lads on your bayonets. Let them mingle with you; let them know the men they have to deal with' (reminding them of a drill they had practised where each man in the rank stabbed at the opponent to his right as he lifted his sword arm). When the two armies were facing each other at a range of about 500 yards on the Jacobite right and about 800 on its left, a cannonade was begun from both sides. Only one set of guns, the Royal Artillery's, were of standard gauges and served by trained gunners. Closely packed on a field that was too narrow, the Jacobite ranks were shredded, round after round, minute by minute. Prince Charles was seen to change his station; shortly afterwards the rebel artillery slackened and ceased. The officers and men in the Jacobite front line had to fight their growing fury as they made efforts to form up around the swathes of men who had been shot down. The redcoats failed to advance — there was no point since the roundshot from their cannon was doing the work for them.

As Brevet-Colonel Belford's men made ready with grapeshot to resist a charge, Cumberland brought forward his cavalry, for cover on his right flank, and to enter the Culwhiniac enclosures behind the Campbell militia on the

The battle of Culloden. An Incident in the Rebellion of 1745, by David Morier. The artist was permitted to use Jacobite prisoners as models for the painting. (The Royal Collection© Her Majesty Queen Elizabeth II)

The Duke of Cumberland as he appeared to admirers (top) and critics (bottom), after the battle of Culloden. When the idea was put forward that the duke become a freeman of one of the London Guilds, a wag replied, 'Let it be of the Butchers', and the epithet stuck. (Both: National Library of Scotland; on loan to the Scottish National Portrait Gallery)

other. This was the only attack the king's army made in the battle, and it met nothing more dangerous than four-foot dry-stane dykes. With the militiamen acting as a demolition squad for the dragoons, their sudden thrust turned the farm into a small fortress looking onto the battlefield. When Wolfe's regiment formed a line part of the way up its outer boundary, the Highlanders would have to brave front and side fire to approach the enemy, and were already having to hold off cavalry in their rear. Nonetheless, by this time they were clamouring to attack out of desperation. Several of the regimental commanders sent messages to the prince, who now had no overview, asking for the order to be given. It seems that he was delaying to give John Roy Stewart time to attempt an outflanking move across the River Nairn. He gave the order to attack several times, only to see the messenger killed. After Lachlan Maclachlan's son was decapitated while carrying it, Brigadier Stapleton took the order to the right wing himself — too late for the Mackintoshes in the centre: they had already burst forward.

As Maxwell noted, 'the only chance the Prince had for a victory that day, was a general shock of the whole line at once' — but, in the event, its slant meant that the advance of the Jacobite front line on the British army resembled a creaking farm gate. Confusion over orders, blinding smoke from the artillery, and the bogginess of much of the ground did not help, and it was unfortunate that the regiments on the left which had furthest to go — the Macdonalds — were thoroughly demoralised, and failed to engage the enemy at all. However, the weight of shot from the artillery and the muskets of the British centre-left also played its part. Under its impact, the Frasers, Stewarts and Camerons in the centre veered to their right, and all the strain was thrown on the makeshift wing: the Atholl men. After being picked off on the charge by the Campbell militia and Wolfe's men, the cramped Atholl brigade plunged through Barrel's and Munro's frontal fire and broke in among them. Without avail — Barrel's regiment, which took the brunt of the assault, was an old one with a good spirit; it was no readier to run than it had been at Falkirk. The sight of it being hacked apart might have encouraged the clans on the left and speeded their advance. Instead, it bulged and fell back, and as the soldiers of the Atholl brigade jammed forward they were impaled on the bayonets of Bligh's and Sempill's in the second line; many of those at the rear were shot down in the torrent of iron from the flanks.

The Highland charge stalled. Everywhere that the clansmen came within range of the levelled muskets, mounds of dead and wounded built up in front of the British lines. Perhaps because they could not see for smoke, like most of the attackers, the men of Clan Chattan had thrown away their firearms. Helpless and furious at being baulked they stood off and hurled stones. Some battalions made feints in a desperate attempt to draw the enemy forward. The redcoats kept shooting, resisting all temptation to break their formation. So few Highlanders escaped the hail of fire and pierced the British ranks that their names and exploits are remembered individually; those who did perished almost to a man. The disgruntled Macdonalds, who found themselves a sprint behind the rest, halted and watched as the moor was turned into a killing field. Moments later a retreat began. There was no alternative.

One English soldier, Alexander Taylor of the Royals, later wrote to his wife that the Highlanders 'came running upon our front-line like troops of hungry wolves, and fought with intrepidity'. The official account published in the *London Gazette* on 26 April emphasised the efficiency with which disciplined firing held the hated enemy at bay:

> Upon the Right, where his Royal Highness had plac'd himself…they came down three several Times within a Hundred Yards of our Men, firing their Pistols and brandishing their Swords; but the Royals and *Pulteney*'s hardly took their firelocks from their Shoulders, so that after those faint Attempts they made off.

The account also emphasises how effectively the king's infantry on the left began the task of stabbing the life out of the rebellion:

> There was scarce a Soldier or Officer of *Barrel*'s, and that Part of *Monroe*'s which engaged, who did not kill one or two Men each with their Bayonets and Spontoons [half-pikes].

Officially sanctioned accounts did not dwell on what happened after the Jacobite army fell back and men began to scatter off the field. The horse, it was noted, 'galloped up briskly, and falling in with the fugitives, did excellent execution. The rest the reader is to guess.' Eighteenth-century readers familiar with public executions were in a position to guess, of course. Cutting in on both flanks and almost encircling the defeated army, Cumberland's mounted troops came into their own as executioners; while, at a heavy cost to themselves, the Irish pickets and the few Jacobite cavalry made heroic efforts to screen the fleeing clans, and some commanders, like Keppoch and Lord Strathallan, died attempting vain counter-attacks. The dragoons had little need or relish to confront the few men who remained steady. The moor was seething with easy targets for their blood lust: many without weapons and some wounded. The mounted men (some of them — Kingston's — volunteers) rode down their quarry, hacking and slashing at anyone they came across in isolation. Battalions which kept together fared best, particularly those which crossed the Nairn and made south; only speed of foot or sheer luck saved those wretches who headed west to Inverness and beyond. They were flung together with the onlookers who had come to watch the battle, and both fled away in panic. It made no difference to the cavalry: soldiers, townsfolk, camp-followers, ghouls, men and women, even a few children — they were cut down indiscriminately. By evening the four miles or so of the road to Inverness was strewn with corpses.

Watching the battle from near the corner of the Culwhiniac enclosures, Prince Charles was plunged into shock at the sight of men he had thought invincible streaming past him in fear of their lives. When he attempted to rally them with a defiant, last-ditch charge, O'Sullivan intervened; the bridle of the prince's horse was seized by an aide, and he was chaperoned off the

Privates of the 8th (top) and 10th (bottom) regiments of Dragoons, painted for the Duke of Cumberland by David Morier in 1751. (The Royal Collection© Her Majesty Queen Elizabeth II)

field by a few of his Lifeguards. There is a tradition that Lord Elcho shouted after him, 'There you go for a damned cowardly Italian.' By the time the British army crossed the field and grounded its weapons later in the afternoon the prince was out of harm's way, but still close enough to hear its roar of triumph. His brief foray as a field-marshal had ended in disaster.

8 THE AFTERMATH

Whatever airs the French may give themselves, and tho' they may easily amuse some of our ignorant giddy people, I can hardly believe they can ever persuade the Pretender's Son to come over again. So much difficulty he had to govern the People he had in arms formerly, so much hardship he has suffered in every shape, that I must conclude him a madman if he ventures again. However, it is very prudent to have a sharp look out.
(ARCHIBALD CAMPBELL OF STONEFIELD TO THE EARL OF ALBERMARLE, 11 FEBRUARY 1747)

UNLIKE many of the battles fought during the War of the Austrian Succession, Culloden was small in scale, brief in duration, and was to prove decisive. The Highlanders' one tactic, the charge, having at last failed them, the Marquis d'Eguilles held no further hopes: 'The prince was vanquished in an instant, never was a defeat more complete than his.' Nor did Lord Lovat. When, on the night after the battle, Charles turned up at his house at Gorthleck on Loch Mhor, Lovat was astonished that the Jacobites had offered battle in such a condition. His advice to the prince was to return to France and raise forces there. As Charles had never entertained the idea of a guerilla campaign, word from Ruthven that a contingent of his routed army was gathering nearby was of little interest to him — particularly as, on the 17th, Lord George, who had made his own way to Badenoch, wrote a rancorous letter to the prince reiterating his part in events leading up to the débâcle. Since one of his Irish familiars had thought fit to remind the prince of how, in similar circumstances, the Scots had handed over his great-grandfather, Charles I, to the English, he was already anxious enough about his situation; Murray's letter only made him more restive and bitter. Believing that the situation in Scotland was irretrievable, Charles sent a message in effect dismissing those who had served him, and bid each man seek his own safety.

The prince set out for the west coast via Invergarry, knowing very little of the misery he had left behind him. While it was clear to both sides that the casualties included the colonels of several clan regiments, along with large numbers of their kin and followers, as the powder-blackened and blood-spattered government soldiers surveyed the weird horror of slaughter while they chewed the food that was brought to them from the ships in the Moray Firth, it seemed sufficient to reckon the victory in terms of the hundreds of bent and bloodied bayonets they had wielded, and no formal count of casualties among the Jacobites was ever made. Unreliable estimates (made by

The Act of Attainder which came into force against 41 leading rebels in June 1746. The first name on the list was that of Alexander, Earl of Kellie, the last that of 'William Fidler, Clerk in the Auditor's Office in the Exchequer of Scotland'. Kellie was commonly thought mad, but had the wit to remark that, it 'maun be a wise government indeed, who begins its act with a Fool and ends with a Fidler'. (National Library of Scotland, Blk.8(18))

Satirical engraving. In The True Contrast, *Prince Charles is portrayed as the 'Fright'ned Italian Bravo', while the Duke of Cumberland is the 'Royal British Hero'. (National Library of Scotland; on loan to the Scottish National Portrait Gallery)*

victorious generals) put the number of insurgents killed at up to 2000. The dazed Jacobites put their own losses higher still at 3000 out of the 5000 believed to have taken the field. The number killed 'mopping up' may have more than doubled the 750 bodies which an army surgeon reckoned lay on the field itself, and he was probably hampered in his efforts by the fact that the corpses lay in heaps. No one else was counting. Attention was focused, instead, on the 326 native rebels who were taken prisoner in and around Inverness, and over 220 men in French uniform who were allowed to surrender together under the gallant Brigadier Stapleton (who died of wounds a few days later). The British army acknowledged its own losses at fifty men killed and nearly 260 wounded out of a complement of around 9000.

On Monday 21 April, the *Edinburgh Evening Courant* reported that, 'Late on Saturday Night the agreeable News of his Royal Highness the Duke's obtaining a compleat Victory over the Rebels, arrived here...Accounts were no sooner received, than Orders were given to the Castle to fire a round of the Great Guns, which was accordingly done early on the Sunday Morning,

112

LIST of the Rebel Prisoners received into Custody by [Edinburgh, Canongate] Keeper of the Goal of the said Place.

Time when taken.	Place where and by whom.	When received into Custody.	From whom.	Prisoners Names.	Quality.	Of what Country Place.	In whose Service and Re[...]

and was returned by Discharges from the Men of War…' The following day the *Courant* was able to confirm details:

> The Particulars which we have hitherto learned are, That the Battle did not last above Half an Hour, during which Time no Quarter was given on either Side, and was exceeding bloody; That 1000 of the Rebels lay dead upon the Spot, and about 200 were killed and wounded on the King's Side. Capt. Grasset is killed, Col. Rich is wounded. The Regiments which distinguished themselves most were Barrel's and Monro's; and it is particularly remarked, that the Scots Regiments behaved with an extraordinary Bravery.

The victory was officially celebrated at Glasgow on the Monday:

> At Ten in the Forenoon the Musick Bells were play'd, and a large Bonfire lighted at the Cross; in the Afternoon the whole Bells of the City were rung; and the Magistrates, accompanied by the Right Hon. the Earl of Dundonald, William Muir, Esq; Member of Parliament for the County of Renfrew, and several other Persons of Distinction, Gentlemen of the University, and principal Inhabitants of the City, went to the Top of the Stair leading to the Town's great Hall, where they drank (under a Discharge of Fire Arms, by a Detachment of the Town's Regiment, which was in his Majesty's Service in the Action near Falkirk) the Healths of his Majesty, their Royal Highnesses the Prince and Princess of Wales, the Duke of Cumberland, all the Branches of the Royal Family, and Success to his Majesty's Arms.

A page from the Edinburgh jail register for 1746. Nationally, between 1745 and 1747, some 3471 prisoners were detained as Jacobites, some on suspicion, others 'in actual rebellion'. Circulars were sent to the Keepers of the various jails, instructing them to prepare and maintain separate records, and authorising a subsistence payment of 4d per day per man, 8d for the sick, and 6s 8d to a surgeon, 'for the Cure of each Man'. (National Library of Scotland, MS.288, f.63)

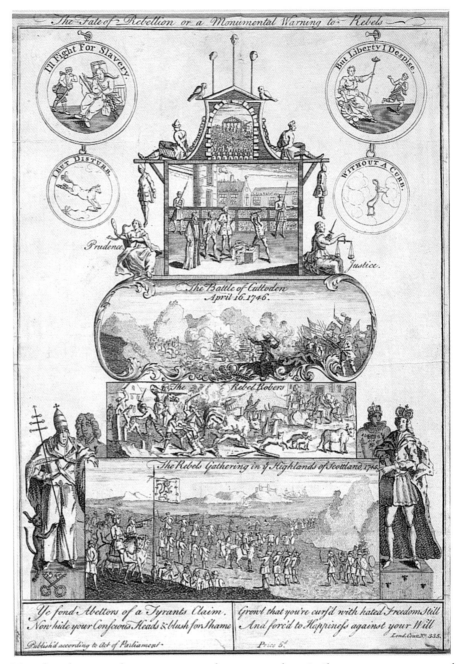

The Fate of Rebellion or a Monumental Warning to Rebels. *(National Library of Scotland; on loan to the Scottish National Portrait Gallery)*

Two days later, as the newspapers also reported, a similar scene was repeated at Edinburgh, which extended its blessing to:

> Our brave Generals, our vigilant Admirals, the Ministers of State, the Friends of the Government, Liberty, Religion and Property…At Night the Loyalty of the Citizens appeared in a manner not to be described…The Illuminations were not only splendid, but decorated in a surprising Manner. The Windows had W. D. C. and VICTORY, DELIVERER OF GREAT BRITAIN; and in some *Justice* was represented trampling *Rebellion* under Foot, and striking her Sword into its Bowel…The Castle play'd Sky Rockets, and during the whole Night all was Mirth, Gayety and unusual Satisfaction.

When it reached London, the news of a victory was all the more welcome because it seemed so complete. Bells were rung, bonfires were lit, windows illuminated and toasts drunk; loyal addresses were composed and parliament acted to increase the Duke of Cumberland's allowances from £15,000 to £40,000 per year. The *Westminster Journal* saw the campaign as nearing its end:

> One great defeat such as the rebels in *Scotland* received from his royal highness, must be fatal and ruinous. Ten such affairs as those at *Preston-Pans* and *Falkirk*, had they preceded the battle of *Culloden*, could not have been of the least service in keeping up their spirits, or engaging others to repair their loss. Insurrections against an established government, let them grow to ever so great a head, if they once meet with a stop, a check, a singular disappointment, are within a little of being totally suppressed.

In the hours which followed the carnage, and in its vicinity, this was less clear. There were many on both sides who were prepared to consider victory or defeat as sufficient unto the day only. By the end of the week, as many as 1500 angry, battered Scots converged on Ruthven; and the coming months were to demonstrate just how great was the Duke of Cumberland's fear of leaving the root of rebellion to grow in Highland soil. That fear had poisoned his attitude to Scotland and to Scots, and it survived Culloden. Eventually, it helped ensure that that the '45 brought to an end the series of intermittent civil wars, fought in part over the issue of Stuart prerogative, which had begun in the late 1630s — but only after terrible retribution. The butchery after Culloden of many hundreds of stragglers and onlookers — and the cold-blooded slaughter of wounded men in the following days — by a corps of officers and common soldiers infected with that fear, marked not the end of an ugly campaign of repression, but the beginning of a new one.

It quickly leaked out that very few wounded Jacobites had survived Culloden. At a gathering in London on 1 May, just a few days after George II had rewarded him with 1000 guineas for bringing news of a victory and of his son's safety, Lord Bury was publicly embarrassed by an inquiry on the subject. Rumours circulated in Scotland that in addition to the wounded men

A letter sent to the National Journal *in May 1746, inquiring about the fate of wounded Jacobites after the battle of Culloden. (National Library of Scotland, MS.2960, f.138)*

left on the field who were shot, clubbed and bayoneted to death within hours, others were burned alive days later in the huts where they had taken refuge, and two groups of wounded officers were driven from shelter and put before firing squads. There were rumours, too, of crimes committed against the people of the countryside, ranging from murderous assaults to theft, obscene acts perpetrated on corpses, and the humiliation of the living. It appeared that prisoners were being treated worse than livestock, kept nearly naked in their own filth without heat or light, and denied medical treatment and food. The commanders at Inverness were not receptive to criticism. When the two leading baillies of Inverness (both Whigs) visited Cumberland's headquarters to recommend clemency for those in custody, they were kicked down a flight of stairs on the orders of men who believed that the rebels deserved severe punishment and were convinced that the future security of the realm necessitated it. It was not to persuade the public, merely to reap the benefit of inflaming their own men, that copies of rebel orders were disclosed which contained instructions to 'give no quarter to the Elector's troops on any account whatsoever'. Inverness simply was not the place to raise the doubts some informed Scots had about the authenticity of the documents, and the improbability of a man like Lord George Murray authorising slaughter. (As the *Caledonian Mercury* reminded its readers when the rebels occupied Edinburgh, the Whigs were the perpetrators, and a Highland clan the victims, of the most infamous example of conduct of that kind: the massacre of Glencoe in 1692.) Such scepticism only added to the victors' belief that Scotland was riddled with Jacobitism.

All ranks in the British army were aware that, in time of war, the bulk of the population were as unlikely to take exception to the chastising of what were seen as savages inhabiting the remote wilderness of the Scottish Highlands, as to the suppression of a revolt among the negroes of Jamaica in late 1744, whatever the means used. The lower ranks were aware too that the fact that the king's son condoned vigorous methods was the best protection against scrutiny from any quarter, and they took full advantage. Many read into their orders a licence to indulge their impulse for revenge and their greed for gain. With

The Lyon in Mourning. Some of Robert Forbes's correspondents sent him swatches of Prince Charles's clothes and decorations, including the dress he wore as 'Betty Burke', and fragments of the oars used to row him across the Minch — which Forbes pasted onto the endpapers of several volumes of the manuscript. (National Library of Scotland, Adv.MS.32.6.18)

rancour from the top helping to create a climate of persecution, honourable men from both nations were placed in a difficult position. The story is preserved of the young Major James Wolfe's refusal at Culloden to execute the wounded Charles Fraser of Inverallochie, acting commander of the Fraser regiment, thus forcing General Hawley to find a private soldier to do the deed (and no doubt incurring his considerable displeasure). More prosaically, with the Duke of Cumberland refusing to allow into his presence any of the handful of his own captured officers who declined to break their word of honour to the rebels, at least one affray resulted between Scots and English officers, with sword-play threatened, following careless remarks from the latter which failed to distinguish between 'Scot' and 'Jacobite'.

While army officers who showed humanity towards wounded men and prisoners could not even be named in print without jeopardising their position, it remained dangerous to publicise what was happening. It was left to the Reverend Robert Forbes, Episcopal minister at Leith and an ardent (if frustrated) Jacobite, patiently to gather evidence from witnesses. Over a period of years he compiled *The Lyon in Mourning* — ten black-edged manuscript volumes of material on the rebellion and its aftermath. It catalogued how the supposedly hot-blooded and random misdeeds after Culloden evolved into systematic and widespread repression. Attempts were made later to deny some of the atrocities brought to light, but the organised rapine could hardly be denied. James Wolfe appears less favourably in the complaint sent to Forbes on behalf of an Aberdeenshire lady, whose husband, George Gordon of Hallhead, had acted as secretary to Lord Pitsligo. It involved the conduct of General Hawley when he was quartered in her house before the army marched to Inverness, and shows that the looting which followed Culloden merely intensified that which preceded it:

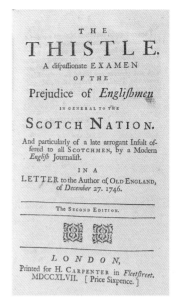

The '45 created a climate of suspicion and hostility towards Scots and Scotland in London. It was still in evidence when John Stuart, 3rd Earl of Bute, became prime minister in 1762. (National Library of Scotland, Ry.1.2.85(25))

> [On the second day] Major Wolfe, came to me, and after asking if I was Mrs Gordon…he said that he was come to tell me that by the Duke of Cumberland and General Hawley's order I was deprived of everything I had except the cloaths upon my back. After delivering this message he said that General Hawley having enquired into my character…I might have any particular thing that I had a mind to and could say was my own. I then desired to have my tea, but the major told me it was very good, and that tea was scarce in the army, so he did not believe I could have it. The same answer was made me when I asked for my chocolate. I mentioned several other things, particularly my china. That, he told me, was, a great deal of it very pretty, and that they were very fond of China themselves, but as they had no ladies travelled with them I might perhaps have some of it. I then desired to have my pictures. He said he supposed I would not wish to have them all. I replied that I did not pretend to name any except my son's. He asked me if I had a son, where he was? I said I had sent him into the country to make room for them…He asked, How old my son was. I said about fourteen. Fourteen, said he, then he is not a child and you will be made to produce him.

Copy of a letter from Lord Lovat, to the Duke of Cumberland, 16 June 1746. Writing in custody at Fort William, Lovat pleads with the duke that he 'did more essential Service to your Royal Family, in suppressing the great Rebellion in 1715...than any of my Rank in Scotland'; and reminds him that, 'I often carried your Royal Highness in my Arms, in the Parks of Kensington and Hampton-Court, to hold you up to your Royal Grandfather, that he might embrace you.' Cumberland later attended his trial and saw him condemned to death. (National Library of Scotland, RB.m.400)

Forbes was supplied with a list two pages long itemising what was packed up and taken from the house, from a dinner service to a horse's bridle. (Wolfe, though, made sure the woman was left her son's picture — minus its frame.)

*****

Only a tiny number of people in Scotland were in a position to urge restraint on the military. The foremost amongst them, Duncan Forbes of Culloden ('King Duncan' as he was known when he served the Walpole administration), was keen to preserve the rule of law in the midst of turmoil. He feared the future consequences of measures which punished the innocent as well as the guilty. He urged Cumberland, 'No severity that is necessary ought to be dispensed with, the omitting such severities is cruelty to the king and kingdom. Unnecessary severities create pity, and pity from unnecessary severities is the most dangerous nurse to disaffection, especially if continued for any time.' The difficulty for Forbes was that the duke had consulted London after Lord Milton gave him similar advice in March, and was assured he had the authority 'to do whatever is necessary for suppressing this unnatural rebellion'.

Cumberland looked on Scottish law and practice as having failed the United Kingdom. He blamed the current upheavals on legal constraints which had made it impracticable to exact proper revenge for the risings of 1715 and 1719. It was common knowledge, for instance, that some senior lawyers had exploited the law's procedural complexity to obstruct the work of the Commissioners of Inquiry into the forfeited estates after the '15; and that, when many of the estates were subsequently sold to the York Buildings Company, the mixed fortunes it enjoyed could be traced in part to legal difficulties in ascertaining the debt burden which was attached to the estates, and also to the ease with which, in a depressed market, the leases could pass into unsuitable hands. Moreover, when Charles landed in Moidart in 1745 there was dismay among Whigs when it was found that there were legal obstacles to raising troops quickly to oppose him. The young Cumberland was shrewd enough to see that the treason statutes and Scottish land laws were pulling on different ropes. The clan system prevalent in the Scottish Highlands and Islands conspicuously failed to promote industry and prosperity; instead, poor land being poorly farmed produced a beggar-thy-neighbour economy, which provided an incentive for men to keep in arms under powerful chieftains, and none to yield to improvement. Under a semi-feudal constitution (reformed in England in 1661) some impoverished chieftains wielded powers greater than those of an English high court judge or the colonel of a British regiment. They were entitled to hold their own courts and, except for a few pleas reserved to the crown, they represented — without training and quite unchecked — what law there was in many large areas, and derived great influence from this power. Cumberland was determined to confront this anomaly head on. Legislation would take time and was for the future. What concerned him most in the interim was the chieftains' ability to force men into arms to pursue their own resentments. He was prepared to act outwith the existing law and to use all the force necessary to curtail this power, and he could only conceal his irritation with Forbes's approach for so long. He referred to Forbes privately as 'that old woman who talked to me of humanity', and eventually blew up at one or other of his cavils: 'The laws, my lord! By G—, I'll make a brigade give laws!'

When he set up his headquarters at Fort Augustus there was the barest pretence of a legal sanction for military severity. It was used openly in an attempt to break the power of the most conspicuous offenders by depopulating their glens and islands, and taking away or destroying everything that could support life in them. (Ironically, Cumberland was much taken with Forbes's suggestion that some clans should be banished, as the only certain way of quelling them — the privy council, though, disagreed.) The policy was being carried out against the small, self-contained communities of the Inner Hebrides and the west coast even before the battle of Culloden was fought. The laird's bailiff penned a record of events on Canna:

> Upon the 3d of April 1746, Lieutenant Thomas Brown, an Irish gentleman with a command of 80 men, did sail with a tender from the *Baltimore* man of war by Captain Fergusons order...came to the haven of Canna, and after sending for James M'Donald, bailie of the Island, and uncle to Glenaladal, told him he was sent by Captains Ferguson and Dove for some fresh beef and mutton, vizt. 20 fat cows and so many wedders. The gentleman asking his orders was answered he would show him no commission of that kind...[T]he flower of the Islanders was with the Prince; soe that the bailie judged it safer both for himself and inhabitants to grant his request...But being wind-bound for 4 days in Canna harbour, behold! they complained to the said bailie the beef of the cattle slaughter'd stunk, and that the country should give them the same number over again. The bailie reckoned this both unjust and cruel...Upon which the officer was petted and said with a rage he knew where and by whom he woud be served...So he hurls away his 60 armed men, gathers all the cattle of the Isle into a particular creek, shot 60 of the best dead, threw the old beef overboard and woud not allow the poor distressed owners to finger a gobbet of it, no not a single tripe.

A few weeks later the women of the island were obliged 'to climb and hide themselves in grottos and in the hollow of hideous precipices that were somewhat unaccessable' when they were warned of a planned mass rape — 'sculking in a starving condition till the men of war sail'd off'.

On 4 June 1746 an Act of Attainder passed into law which gave the authorities power to arrest and summarily execute any one of forty-one named individuals and confiscate their property. Some of those on the list were dead already and few of the leading figures in the rebellion were to fall into their hands. (Of the Scottish peers who did, the Earl of Kilmarnock and Lord Balmerino were the only ones who fought at Culloden. Lord Cromarty was detained in Sutherland on the eve of the battle, and Lord Lovat was betrayed while hiding in a tree. The English 'Earl' of Derwentwater was captured on a voyage from France.) Instead, vengeance was wreaked on the homes of those who went into hiding or withheld arms, including a great many common men.

The islanders of Eigg were punished severely for infringing the Disarming Act. They had surrendered weapons and were given receipts for them, but more were found on the island on 20 June when the authorities came to conduct a search for a wanted man, Captain John Macdonald. He was taken, and then used to persuade the islanders to come forward and comply with the Act. They did so, not knowing that:

> There was a devilish paper found about him, containing a list of all the Eigg folk that were in the Princes service...so that there were noe fewer than 38 snatched aboard the man of war, were brought to London, from thence transported to Jamaica...Many of them dyed and starved ere they arrove at the Thames. The most of them were married men, leaving throng families behind them. They slaughtered all their cattle, pillaged all their houses ore they left the isle, and ravished a girl or two.

General Hawley confessed to having 7000 cottages burnt and wondered if it was enough. As Prince Charles was to discover for himself when he returned to the mainland from the Hebrides in July, in some glens no people, no shelter and nothing edible was left.

*****

As spring turned into summer the cost of withdrawing so many regiments from the Low Countries was made painfully clear to the high command. Outnumbering allied forces by more than two to one, the French followed up their successes of 1745 by taking Brussels in late February, and moved successfully against Louvain (6 May), Antwerp (21 May) and then Mons (10 July). Further losses would follow, forcing the Dutch to reconsider their role in the conflict. Although the war had been taking that course even before British forces were evacuated, the rebellion undoubtedly made the position worse; the dishonour to their arms was yet another stick for officers and men to take to the Highlanders when search parties were sent into all the rebel glens. As well as looking for weapons, they were under orders to break or burn the Highlanders' farm implements and domestic utensils (crude as they were), and drive off their livestock. The common run of soldiers greedily joined their officers in pocketing the gains from a mart in confiscated cattle held at Fort Augustus (which was lucrative enough to draw dealers from as far afield as the north of England); while the worst elements in the army took advantage of the isolation to strip, rape or even murder some of the unprotected women they came across. Even the soldiers' recreations gave offence locally: horse races organised to lift the spirits of men depressed by the mountain environment led to rumours of great sums being wagered and lost, and added to the redcoats' reputation for iniquity.

By contrast, as they made their way from Edinburgh to Aberdeen, the men in Cumberland's army must have been struck by how familiar and 'civilised' was the way of life in the towns and counties east of the Grampians. The many Jacobites here were not the wild and strange-seeming Gaels of the central and western Highlands and Islands, nor were they Catholics in the main, but Episcopalians or Non-Jurants. When, after Culloden, a force under the Earl of Ancram returned to mete out punishment, the scope for action was that much more limited in consequence. Reprisals were devised which played on enmity between the different religions; efforts were concentrated on the destruction of the dissenters' chapels, libraries and seminaries. Perhaps because sympathy nevertheless lingered among some Presbyterians for the plight of their persecuted neighbours, the military authorities in Edinburgh eventually decided to force ministers of the Church of Scotland to take sides; they were compelled to supply lists of those in their parishes who were 'out' in the rebellion, to supplement lists of prisoners drawn up by Excise officers. Men like Captain Carolina Scott and Major Lockhart of the army, and Captain John Fergusson of the navy are remembered for their cruelties against their countrymen in the western Highlands and Islands, but petty avengers emerged too, as the Reverend John Skinner of Aberdeenshire confirmed to Robert Forbes in 1749:

Lords Kilmarnock and Balmerino, from a print which went on sale after their execution on 18 August 1746. (National Library of Scotland; on loan to the Scottish National Portrait Gallery)

> When our meeting[-house] was burnt the officer of dragoons came to my house in quest of me, but mist me. After that I was often alarm'd, but never in danger till July 29 that Hardy and 6 of Loudon's regiment came to my house. I was that day at Rora baptising a child or so, and came not home till pretty late when to my surprize I found 7 armed men at my wife's bedside who had lien in about 10 days before, and had not yet left her bed. I ask'd the fellow, Hardy, what he wanted here, on which in great confusion he told me I was the King's prisoner and behov'd to go to Aberdeen. This was Tuesday night, and I was oblig'd to go under two screw'd bayonets to Mr. Brown's for a letter to Hardy to let me stay at my own house till Friday...While I was at Brown's they had packed up all my shirts and stockings, most of my books, with several other bits of portable furniture, and 10 shillings sterling of money, and carry'd it off to Brown's, where they deposited all as in a place of shelter. Thus I was left naked except what was on my back, and Brown, like a good Christian and clergyman, reseted chearfully all that the ruffians plunder'd me of.

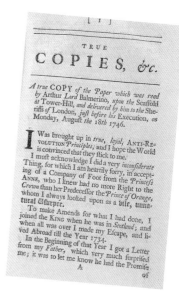

Lord Balmerino was a Jacobite by conviction; throughout his trial and execution his composure and his robust defence of his principles compelled admiration from onlookers. (National Library of Scotland, Ry.1.2.85)

✻✻✻✻✻

A month after Culloden the privy council decided that all prosecutions for treason should be undertaken in England. Thirty-two deserters from the British army had been condemned at drum-head courts and were hanged at Inverness on or after 20 April, and a few spies were summarily executed;

The trial of Lord Lovat before both Houses of Parliament assembled in Westminster Hall, 9-18 March 1747. Lovat is the central figure in black in the foreground. (National Library of Scotland; on loan to the Scottish National Portrait Gallery)

none of the rebels were executed in Scotland however. After the early rejoicing, public ceremonial in the Scottish capital centred around the destruction of sixteen clan standards, which were burned at intervals throughout June by the city's chimney-sweeps, and a brief stopover by the Duke of Cumberland on his return south from Fort Augustus on 21 July. It was a different story in London. After handing over the command in Scotland to the (reluctant) Earl of Albemarle, Cumberland arrived in London on 25 July to a hero's welcome. The celebrations after Culloden were renewed and even surpassed; Handel wrote 'The Conquering Hero' for the duke, a flower was renamed the 'Sweet William' in his honour, gifts and offices were bestowed on him, and crowds flocked around him wherever he went. His arrival coincided with the public execution at Kennington Common of the leading English rebels who had surrendered at Carlisle; they had been brought to London under new powers which enabled the crown to appoint the place of a trial. Although the total of eighty men executed as traitors represented just over two per cent of the 3471 prisoners in government hands, their deaths succeeded, as intended, in casting a macabre shadow over the summer of 1746. The lesson was aimed principally at an English, rather than a Scots audience and, to that end, the Manchester Regiment was punished out of proportion to its numbers, with twenty four men receiving the death-sentence. Francis Townley was the first of nine on whom the grim threats of the statute were carried out on 30 July, as that month's edition of the *Gentleman's Magazine* vividly recorded:

> When they had hung about five minutes, Mr *Townley* was cut down, his body (not being quite dead) being stripp'd and laid on the block, the hangman with a cleaver severed his head from his body, which were put into a coffin; then taking out the bowels and heart, threw them into the fire: he then proceeded to the next, cutting them down, beheading and disbowelling them one by one, in the same manner as the first; when the heart of the last was put into the fire, the executioner cry'd out, *God save K. George*, at which the multitude of spectators gave a great shout.

Just over a fortnight later, on 18 August, Lord Balmerino and the Earl of Kilmarnock were beheaded on Tower Hill, following widely reported trials before the assembled lords in Westminster Hall. (Lord Cromarty was reprieved after his wife had fainted at King George's feet.) Other executions of lesser rebels took place at Carlisle (nineteen), Brampton (seven), Penrith (seven) and York (twenty-four). The fact that large numbers of Jacobites were not tried did not mean that they escaped punishment — merely that the authorities carefully weighed the trouble and expense of securing convictions against the benefits of making an example of selected culprits. They allowed nineteen out of twenty among the lower ranks to escape trial by a process of drawing lots — secure in the knowledge that, for the most part, conditions in the typhus-infected hulks and jails were a horrible punishment in themselves: 772 (over twenty-two per cent of the total) appear to have died from illness or maltreatment in custody. Eventually, 936 were transported to the colonies — with or without convictions. Of the rest, a few, mostly gentlemen, were banished abroad, ninety-two were pardoned on enlisting in the British army, and the remainder (over a third of the total) were in time released, after undergoing a gruesome ordeal. The only ones who fared at all well in custody were those with political connections, and the 387 men in French or Spanish service who were exchanged as prisoners of war.

*****

A conscientious soldier, the Earl of Albemarle was every bit as thorough in the hunt for rebels as his predecessor. Redcoats were seen in areas like Loch Sunart, which had hitherto been considered inaccessible, and every one of the Hebridean islands was searched; some former Jacobites were bribed into spying for the government and others were pressured into becoming informers (the most notorious of whom was John Murray of Broughton, who later gave evidence which helped convict Lord Lovat). However, the prize the army and militia most wanted eluded them. Prince Charles took a boat from Borrodale at the end of April and was carried to the Outer Hebrides by a storm. Had he remained at Borrodale another two days he would have been picked up by two French privateers, *Le Mars* and *La Bellone*. After landing 35,000 *louis d'or* (later to become known as the 'Loch Arkaig treasure', when the bulk of it disappeared in mysterious circumstances), they were just taking on board a group of leading Jacobites, including the Duke of Perth, Lord John Drummond and Lord Elcho, when British warships appeared in Loch nan Uamh and attacked them. Although the French had the better of this, the last battle of the '45, they headed out to sea soon after. The prince was left to his Flight in the Heather, which gave the rising a new and unexpected twist, and altered much subsequent perception of it — not least Charles's own.

As many now knew, provided he could keep faith with himself and his purposes, Charles was capable of shrugging off misfortunes that might distress, or even crush, other people. But even those who viewed this as grounds for criticism must have been surprised at the danger and hardship he withstood throughout a manhunt lasting five months, and involving more than 2000 soldiers and militia. Although he arrived on Benbecula sick and exhausted, when Charles stepped ashore he found himself in his element, in a way that he had not been since the Jacobite army abandoned Derby. Free of obligations and guided by trusty partisans, the life of a stealthy fugitive suited his temperament, and his youthful hunting exploits served him in good stead when it came to foraging off the land. He suffered throughout from scurvy and dysentery and was plagued by midges but, as one of his companions, Macdonnel of Lochgarry observed, his physical resilience was remarkable: 'never was there a Highlander born cou'd travel up and down hills better or suffer more fatigue. Show me a king or prince in Europe cou'd have born the like, or the tenth part of it.'

Flora Macdonald (1722-1790) was the daughter of Ranald Macdonald, a farmer at Milton in South Uist. Her bravery, allied to the fact that, in 1746, her step-father Hugh Macdonald, a covert Jacobite, was commander of the goverment militia on the island, greatly aided Prince Charles's escape from the Hebrides in July of that year. Painted by Richard Wilson, in London, in 1747. (Scottish National Portrait Gallery)

Prince Charles disguised as 'Betty Burke', engraved by J. Williams. (National Library of Scotland; on loan to the Scottish National Portrait Gallery)

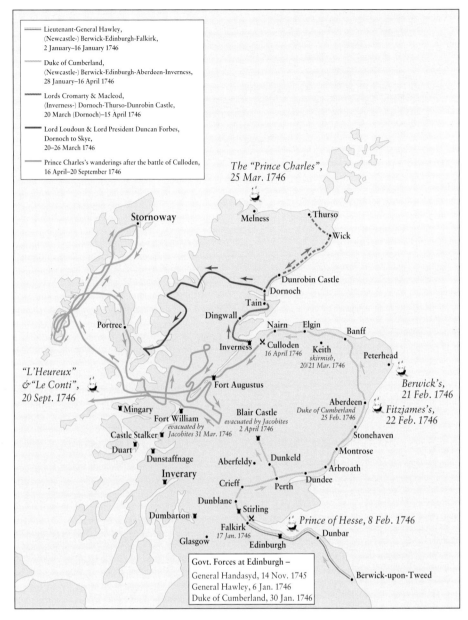

Lieutenant-General Hawley,
(Newcastle-) Berwick-Edinburgh-Falkirk,
2 January–16 January 1746

Duke of Cumberland,
(Newcastle-) Berwick-Edinburgh-Aberdeen-Inverness,
28 January–16 April 1746

Lords Cromarty & Macleod,
(Inverness-) Dornoch-Thurso-Dunrobin Castle,
20 March (Dornoch)–15 April 1746

Lord Loudoun & Lord President Duncan Forbes,
Dornoch to Skye,
20–26 March 1746

Prince Charles's wanderings after the battle of Culloden,
16 April–20 September 1746

The "Prince Charles",
25 Mar. 1746

Stornoway
Melness   • Thurso
• Wick

Dunrobin Castle
Dornoch
Tain
Dingwall
Portree
Nairn • Elgin • Banff
Inverness ✕ Culloden
16 April 1746   Keith
skirmish,
20/21 Mar. 1746   • Peterhead
"L'Heureux"
&"Le Conti",
20 Sept. 1746
Fort Augustus
Berwick's,
21 Feb. 1746
Aberdeen •
Duke of Cumberland
25 Feb. 1746   Fitzjames's,
22 Feb. 1746
Mingary
Fort William
evacuated by
Jacobites 31 Mar. 1746   Blair Castle
evacuated by Jacobites
2 April 1746
Stonehaven
Castle Stalker
Duart   • Montrose
Dunstaffnage   Aberfeldy   Dunkeld
Inverary   • Arbroath
Crieff   Dundee
Dunblane   Perth
Dumbarton   Stirling
✕
Falkirk
17 Jan. 1746   Prince of Hesse, 8 Feb. 1746
Glasgow   Dunbar
Edinburgh
Berwick-upon-Tweed

Govt. Forces at Edinburgh –
General Handasyd, 14 Nov. 1745
General Hawley, 6 Jan. 1746
Duke of Cumberland, 30 Jan. 1746

Operations in Scotland in 1746, including Prince Charles's wanderings, April-September 1746.

He roamed the 'Long Island' of the Hebrides during May and June (including three undisturbed weeks at Glen Coradale in South Uist), left for Skye disguised as Flora Macdonald's fictitious maid 'Betty Burke' on 28 June, spent just over a week there and on Raasay, and evaded capture on the mainland from 7 July until after mid-September. Partly because only a tiny handful of Highlanders coveted the reward on his head, the authorities had little success in tracking him down. There may have been few signs other than nightmares and bouts of increasingly heavy drinking that this moody thoroughbred of a man grieved over the suffering that he had brought to the Highlands, but the loyalty shown to him by many of those who had lost everything in his Cause still arouses admiration, and has never lost its poignancy.

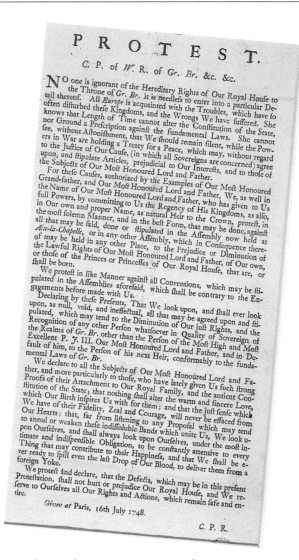

PROTEST.

C. P. of W. R. of Gr. Br. &c. &c.

NO one is ignorant of the Hereditary Rights of Our Royal House to the Throne of Gr. Br. it is needless to enter into a particular Detail thereof. All *Europe* is acquainted with the Troubles, which have so often disturbed these Kingdoms, and the Wrongs We have suffered. She knows that Length of Time cannot alter the Constitution of the State, nor Ground a Prescription against the fundamental Laws. She cannot see, without Astonishment, that We should remain silent, while the Powers in War are holding a Treaty for a Peace, which may, without regard to the Justice of Our Cause, (in which all Sovereigns are concerned) agree upon, and stipulate Articles, prejudicial to Our Interests, and to those of the Subjects of Our Most Honoured Lord and Father.

For these Causes, authorized by the Examples of Our Most Honoured Grand-father, and Our Most Honoured Lord and Father, We, as well in the Name of Our Most Honoured Lord and Father, who has given to Us full Powers, by committing to Us the Regency of His Kingdoms, as also, in Our own and proper Name, as natural Heir to the Crown, protest, in the most solemn Manner, and in the best Form, that may be done, against all that may be said, done or stipulated in the Assembly now held at *Aix-la-Chapelle*, or in any other Place, to the Prejudice or Diminution of may be held in any other Place, to the Prejudice or Diminution of the Lawful Rights of Our Most Honoured Lord and Father, of Our own, or those of the Princes or Princesses of Our Royal House, that are, or shall be born.

We protest in like Manner against all Conventions, which may be stipulated in the Assemblies aforesaid, which shall be contrary to the Engagements before made with Us.

Declaring by these Presents, That We look upon, and shall ever look upon, as null, void, and ineffectual, all that may be agreed upon and stipulated, which may tend to the Diminution of Our just Rights, and the Recognition of any other Person whatsoever in Quality of Sovereign of the Realms of Gr. Br. other than the Person of the Most High and Most Excellent P. J. III. Our Most Honoured Lord and Father, and in Default of him, to the Person of his next Heir, conformably to the fundamental Laws of Gr. Br.

We declare to all the Subjects of Our Most Honoured Lord and Father, and more particularly to those, who have lately given Us such strong Proofs of their Attachment to Our Royal Family, and the antient Constitution of the State; that nothing shall alter the warm and sincere Love, which Our Birth inspires Us with for them; and that the just sense which We have of their Fidelity, Zeal and Courage, will never be effaced from Our Hearts; that, far from listening to any Proposal which may tend to annul or weaken these indissoluble Bands which unite Us, We look upon Ourselves, and shall always look upon Ourselves, under the most intimate and indispensible Obligation, to be constantly attentive to every Thing that may contribute to their Happiness, and that We shall be ever ready to spill even the last Drop of Our Blood, to deliver them from a foreign Yoke.

We protest and declare, that the Defects, which may be in this present Protestation, shall not hurt or prejudice Our Royal House, and We reserve to Ourselves all Our Rights and Actions, which remain safe and entire.

Given at Paris, 16th July 1748.

C. P. R.

In July 1748 Prince Charles protested vigorously to the French government at the inclusion of a clause in the Treaty of Aix-la-Chapelle, requiring the Stuarts to leave French soil, even though he was perfectly aware that the British would not sign the treaty without it, while France could not afford to prolong a ruinous war. (National Library of Scotland; on loan to the Scottish National Portrait Gallery)

Gradually, as other military commitments became pressing, the search for the prince was wound down. Meanwhile, with each new escapade, Charles grew more ebullient, and took to wondering aloud whether or not Providence was preserving him for some great destiny. By the time he crossed the Great Glen heading for his last refuge in Scotland ('Cluny's Cage' above Loch Ericht) he was even giving serious consideration to Lochgarry's scheme for another rising in the hills. With Lord George Murray in hiding near his home, awaiting the opportunity to make his way abroad, it was left to Cluny and Lochiel (whose ankles had been broken at Culloden) to dissuade Charles from an act of folly. A year before, they might have marvelled at the strength of his determination to bring about a coup. In the summer of 1746, there was something chilling about it. When it was heard that two French ships, *L'Heureux* and *Le Prince de Conti* had anchored in Loch nan Uamh to sit out a storm, the prince's party made their way by stages to the coast, and in the early hours of 20 September, Charles set sail for France, accompanied by a body of his supporters. He was never to set foot in Scotland again.

When he arrived at Roscoff on 30 September (Old Style), it was to discover that he was being talked of and admired all over Europe. Suddenly, and

Pastel portrait of Prince Charles in 1748, by Maurice Quentin de La Tour. (Scottish National Portrait Gallery)

overwhelmingly, he found himself the dashing hero of the Paris mob, fêted by Louis XV at Fontainebleau and lionised by the French aristocracy. The legend of the 'Prince in the Heather' sprang up, and, for a time, in the midst of this dazzling success, it almost seemed as if the dismal failure at Culloden had been forgotten…but not quite. There was genuine admiration for his feats at Louis' court, but, in a country so badly divided as France then was, it was also politic for ministers to make a fuss over a popular figure like Charles — for a time, at any rate. As he was to discover when he tried to convert his celebrity into the harder currency of arms and money for another expedition, avid curiosity, warm sympathy and a certain amount of martial fervour among the ladies fell considerably short of the heartfelt thanks for its deliverance which a grateful nation had shown to his portly rival across the Channel.

His dismay often giving way to fury, Charles spent much of the next two years striving to collect the debt which he believed Louis XV owed him. It became clearer with each passing month that, with a European peace in prospect, there was little or no place in French policy for another rising, but, characteristically, it only made him more determined. In his efforts to embarrass the king he shed friends, family, many of his supporters, and, eventually, his decorum. His reputation suffered. In December 1748, by which time the increasingly sordid tangle of his personal life had become the stuff of common gossip, he finally succeeded in forcing Louis' hand, but not in the way he had intended. To comply with French obligations under the treaty of Aix-la-Chapelle (which ended the War of the Austrian Succession), Louis had Charles arrested. One night, on his way to the opera, he was waylaid by a party of soldiers, bound with silk cords, bundled into a carriage, and escorted to the border. Charles's attempt to keep his ambitions alive by bearding the King of France in his own capital — probably the most foolish of all his audacious gambles — had failed. Ahead of him lay forty years in exile, during which time Europe looked on as the young and dashing hero he had once been tragically declined into an embittered and ailing alcoholic.

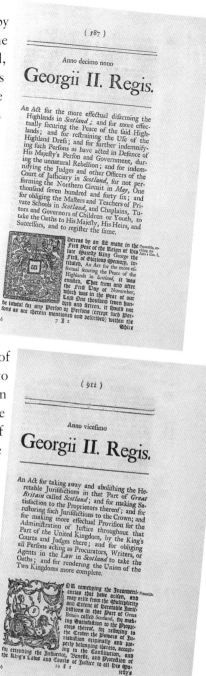

*****

After the 1715 rising, wise counsel had held that the north of Scotland would never be at peace until there was a new kind of Highlander, one who was no longer illiterate, isolated and tied to impoverished hereditary warlords, and some faltering steps had been taken to provide education (secular and religious), improve agriculture and introduce manufactures. The '45 had clearly shown that the pace of change had been too slow, the obstacles to assimilation too great. The majority in the United Kingdom followed the lead of the Protestant churches in rejecting a Stuart restoration, but the Young Pretender's enterprise still held a specious appeal for those clans left at the margin of North Britain economically, and beyond the pale of its established religion. Old loyalties promised rewards that the new ones had failed to deliver. When the rebellion was over, the fact that it had, to some extent, been curtailed because a number of those involved had joined the prince's standard against their better judgment, perhaps argued for quickening the pace of reform rather than abandoning it; but after Culloden the clamour for repression was loud, and ministers tended to share the military's fears that the Hydra might not be dead.

A stringent new Disarming Act was passed on 12 August 1746, and, as far as possible, rigorously enforced. Its provisions went beyond merely depriving the disaffected of weapons. Outwith the king's service, a ban was placed on the peculiar tartan dress of the Highlander, and his accoutrements, which, with other measures to be introduced, amounted to no less than a wide-ranging attack on his culture; attempting anything less, ministers thought, was simply applying a dressing to a septic wound. It never occurred to them that the culture they were bent on destroying might have an intrinsic value. Legislation was passed to abolish the Heritable Jurisdictions (in contravention of the Treaty of Union), and to end tenants' military obligations to landowners; the estates of attainted rebels were

The Disarming Act (19, Geo.II, c.39). (National Library of Scotland)

The Heritable Jurisdictions Act (20, Geo.II, c.43) was passed on 17 June 1747. (National Library of Scotland)

forfeited, and later, in 1752, roughly a quarter of them were annexed 'inalienably' to the crown, under the management of commissioners. In addition, surveys were made and plans drawn for a lengthy and costly programme of building or repairing strongholds (the showpiece of which was the massive new Fort George at Ardersier, begun in 1748 and not completed until 1769 at a cost of £100,000) to be linked by an extensive network of military roads. The Scottish mainland became in effect an occupied country. Yet still the authorities remained worried. The amount of crime being committed by desperate vagabonds from the Jacobite army who had taken to the hills kept alive their worst fears of another rising.

Meanwhile, the social and economic problems peculiar to the Highlands — the archaic relationship of chief to tacksmen and tenants, and of all Highlanders to their fragile subsistence — remained. As the years passed, it was not the so-called Six Acts which altered Highland life, although the endeavours of the Commissioners for the Annexed Estates were important. It was the gradual absorption of the changes which had taken place in the relatively peaceful and law-abiding commercial society which had developed in the Lowlands and beyond — changes which its own poor communications and mostly inward-looking leaders had kept out of the Highlands for considerably more than an eighteenth-century lifetime. Alienation was ended by better roads, more bridges, new towns and harbours, improvements in agriculture, new industries, and, above all, new social relationships and ways of doing business. Stability came, and the Jacobite threat disappeared, long before Prince Charles died in 1788. Dismayed by defeat and the empty promises they felt Charles had lured them with, the Jacobite nobility and gentry gradually rehabilitated themselves, and transferred their allegiance to the crown to gain access to opportunities in its service. (The Master of Lovat set an example which others copied. Despite the fact that his father was executed for treason in March 1747, he raised a regiment of Highlanders for the king during the Seven Years War (1756–1763) and served with distinction

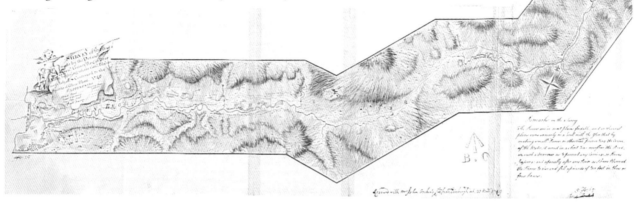

'Brae Marr to Glen-Shee'. A detailed road-map prepared by the Board of Ordnance, showing one of the military roads laid after the '45. (National Library of Scotland, Z3/32a)

in Canada under his old adversary, James Wolfe.) In time, the Highland chieftains would follow their Whig cousins in becoming landowners on the Lowland model, measuring their wealth in money, not in the number of their retainers. Simply by exercising a power they had always possessed, but rarely if ever used, the landowners themselves severed ancient links more effectively than new legislation ever could.

The clearances made by the military in the wake of Culloden were not permanent, and were not in themselves (as is often thought) directly responsible for the creation of what the writer, Ivor Brown, touring the north-western Highlands in the 1950s, referred to as the 'dead vast'. For one thing, the population grew over the following fifteen years, and the travels overseas of soldiers in the newly raised Highland regiments is thought to have been as important an influence as rising prices and food shortages in the phenomenon of emigration which began to be noticed in the 1750s and 60s. However, the aftermath of the '45 bequeathed to British legislators a 'Highland Problem' shorn of its military dimension, but no less intractable for that. It was fatuous to assume that, faced with a harsh landscape, where resources and the means to exploit them were in short supply and concentrated in a few hands, the mutual dependency of master and man in a military caste would give way smoothly to a purely economic relationship. Despite some remarkable achievements, many of the innovations introduced to the Highlands did not 'take', and a few were to be anything but beneficial. The clearances, which began in the late eighteenth and continued into the

Prince Charles aged sixty-four, by Hugh Douglas-Hamilton. (Scottish National Portrait Gallery)

nineteenth century, were to show that the relations between landlords and tenants could be just as pernicious as those between chiefs and vassals.

Viewed in its British context, the rebellion of 1745-6 has a significance beyond that of the mere bursting of a romantic bubble: it was the last occasion on which there was a serious threat to the crown from an army raised within its own borders (at least until the Easter rising in Dublin in 1916), and the extinction of Jacobitism brought to a close an era in which constitutional disputes periodically erupted into armed civil strife. It was superseded by one whose characteristic features were relatively rapid growth in trade and industry, colonial expansion, migration, and territorial wars overseas. Whether the final 'victory' of one value system over another (constitutional monarchy over arbitrary, a mercantile spirit over a feudal, Protestant over Catholic) brought these changes about, or whether new ways were merely the fruits of the new stability — or whether, indeed, change was for the worse — is a debate which still has life in it.

SOURCES FOR THE HISTORY OF THE 'FORTY-FIVE

While it lasted, the Jacobite rebellion was reported fairly accurately, if a little patchily, in the thrice-weekly Edinburgh newspapers, the *Caledonian Mercury* and the *Edinburgh Evening Courant*, and the monthly *Scots Magazine*. When it was over, the presses were used to confirm the dictum that history — published history, at any rate — is written by the victors. For more than a generation, triumphal hack-work histories from approved pens put the government slant on events, unchallenged. Formerly, Jacobites had considered a pride in Scottish history and culture their preserve, but with the severed heads and limbs of former comrades on display a short walk from most publishers' premises, they judged it wiser not to pick up where the hapless John Murray of Broughton's testimony left off. Nevertheless, many former rebels took what steps were available to set the record straight — if only because the crushing of the '45 by no means put an end to the bitter arguments among them which had marred it. While the leading figures in exile on the continent — including the prince himself and Lord George Murray — privately circulated accounts defending their conduct, a number of those remaining in Scotland heard about the Reverend Robert Forbes's activities, and passed information to him for *The Lyon in Mourning*, the compendium of accounts of the rebellion he spent the last twenty-nine years of his life compiling. A few of the exiles who prepared philosophical histories in the French style in the hope of a wider audience were destined to be disappointed. Although Jacobite memoirs later provided historians with a treasure trove, none were published in Britain in the eighteenth century and a tiny few were known abroad. For five decades or more, the '45 owed its place in the popular memory to two activities outside the scope of any official ban: the telling of stories and the singing of songs.

The first reliable narrative of the affair by a participant was the *History of the Rebellion in 1745* by the writer John Home, who, as a young Whig volunteer, had been captured and imprisoned after the battle of Falkirk. This appeared in 1802, and the next twenty-odd years witnessed a change in attitudes. Time played its part: the death of Henry Stuart, Cardinal York in 1807; the extinction of the French threat at Waterloo in 1815 (capping decades of loyal service by Highland regiments in the British army); and, in 1820, the accession of a monarch, George IV, who lacked his predecessors' aversion to Scotland — together these helped bring the Jacobite rebellion in from the cold. As the long Napoleonic wars drew to their close, the advance of the Industrial Revolution was also significant. During this period, like many other processes, printing was being transformed from a craft into an industry, with Edinburgh as one of its principal centres. At the same time that it permitted a rapid increase in the number of good quality magazines and books available to readers, taken as a whole, the introduction of factory methods of production was the harbinger of a new bleakness in Scottish life, and this required its antidote. When Sir Walter Scott (1771-1832) made the rebellion of 1745 the setting for his great historical novel, *Waverley* (1814), the reading public throughout Britain responded with wild enthusiasm, and the fame of the book quickly spread further afield. Its origins may have lain in a mixture of German romanticism, and the vivid exploits told to Scott as a boy by Edinburgh porters and chairmen who were veterans of Prince Charles's battles, but this work of fiction did more than anything else to open the door to serious study of the murky areas of Scotland's past, with the '45 enjoying prominence among them.

The following year a selection of Duncan Forbes's papers were published, the papers of George Lockhart of Carnwath appeared in 1817, and, in 1822, James (Chevalier de) Johnstone's *Memoirs* were printed. In 1824, Sir Walter

Various editions of Sir Walter Scott's Waverley, *including the 'Magnum Opus', with revisions in the author's own hand in preparation for a definitive edition of his works. (National Library of Scotland, MSS.23001-2)*

published *Redgauntlet,* another novel set in the '45. This was followed in 1827 by Robert Chambers's detailed *History of the Rebellion of 1745-6.* Before the decade was out, Scott dealt with the events again at length in his influential *Tales of a Grandfather,* the history of Scotland he wrote late in his life. Based on insights into frictions among leading Jacobites discussed in the manuscript *Narrative* by James Maxwell of Kirkconnell, a captain in the prince's Lifeguards, Scott was highly critical of Prince Charles's shortcomings. Nevertheless, by 1830, amid a general reawakening of interest in Scottish history, culture and traditions, the public's fascination with the '45 was as firm as the ban on it had once been: writers and publishers could barely keep up.

Scott's antiquarian interests made him a prime mover in the prestigious Bannatyne Club, inaugurated in 1823 to put older Scottish texts and records into the press. It acted as the model for others such as the Maitland Club (1828), the Abbotsford (1833) and the Spalding (1839). Through their efforts, and those of the many new printing firms, important sources were made available to historians of the rising. These included Lord George Murray's 'Marches of the Highland Army' (contained in Chambers's *Jacobite Memoirs of the Rebellion of 1745,* 1834); the *Cochrane Correspondence regarding the affairs of Glasgow 1745-46* (Maitland Club, 1836); Maxwell's *Narrative of Charles Prince of Wales's Expedition to Scotland in the Year 1745* (Maitland Club, 1841); and the *Memoirs of Sir Robert Strange and Andrew Lumisden* (1855). J. Browne's *History of the Highlands and of the Highland Clans* appeared in 1848 and 1849, just at the time that Prince Albert's purchase of Balmoral Castle was leading to a new wave of interest in the Highlands. In the second half of the nineteenth century an immense amount of research went into the compilation of detailed Scottish clan and family histories, written by various individuals, but most notably by Sir William Fraser. Among other things, these helped reveal the dilemmas the prince's landing thrust upon individual chiefs, of both persuasions. (See, for example, Fraser's account of the life of Sir Ludovick Grant of Grant, a Hanoverian whose 'country' was surrounded by Jacobite clans.)

By the 1870s the original historical clubs were defunct, but in that decade the Historical Manuscripts Commission began its task of cataloguing manuscript collections in libraries and charter chests the length and breadth of Britain. This inevitably opened up new sources for understanding the Georgian period, including the Stuart Papers (purchased by the government earlier in the century). In 1886 the New Spalding Club was started and, the same year, study of the '45 gained major new impetus when the Scottish History Society was established. It was to bring to light a wide variety of contemporary papers, including several large collections of official documents. *A List of Persons concerned in the Rebellion* (taken from Excise and other records) appeared in 1890, and the publication in full of *The Lyon in Mourning,* in 1895 and 1896, was supplemented, in 1897, by Walter B. Blaikie's indispensable *Itinerary of Prince Charles Edward Stuart,* compiled largely from it. John Murray of Broughton's *Memorials* followed in 1898.

A Selection of Scottish Forfeited Estates Papers appeared in 1909, and an interesting collection of short narratives, account-books etc. in the *Origins of the 'Forty-Five* (1916). The sobering three-volume *Prisoners of the '45* (1928-9) sifted official records to ascertain the fate of those taken into custody during and after the rebellion. Other narratives appeared at intervals in the Society's Miscellanies, such as, in 1926, Father Giulio C. Cordara's *Commentary,* written in 1751 at the behest of Cardinal York. In the 1930s and '40s, acting on their own initiative, the historians Henrietta and Alistair Tayler retrieved a number of manuscripts from obscurity, including, in 1938, John William O'Sullivan's *Narrative* (from among the Stuart Papers), and a decade later Henrietta Tayler edited Prince Charles's own memoir of events (for the Roxburghe Club).

In assessing what had emerged in the previous sixty years, accounts written after the Second World War made good use of material from letters, regimental order books and official papers to make comparisons; although, increasingly, biography appealed as the ideal way of unifying so many diverse sources. Then, in 1971-72, R.C. Jarvis published an influential collection of essays, based on miscellaneous papers, which threw light on a number of unfamiliar areas of the rising, including espionage, intelligence-gathering, and propaganda. In 1975, N. Rogers looked at London court records for 1745-6 and drew up a profile of those arrested for sedition at the time. In 1984 Aberdeen University Press published a *Muster Roll* of the Jacobite army, drawn from a variety of sources. In addition to an in-depth study of the French input to the '45 (1981), F.J. McLynn produced a detailed diary of the Jacobite army in England (1983) along the lines of Blaikie's *Itinerary,* an essay on who the Jacobites were (1985), and the most exhaustive biography to date of Charles Edward Stuart (1988) — which attempts psychological analysis of its subject. His work helped focus attention on the large amount of Jacobite material to be found in the archives of those European states which, at one time or another, supported the Stuarts in exile, including France, Spain and the Vatican. In late 1994, a memoir translated from its original French, and believed to be that of Donald Cameron of Lochiel, was printed in Dr John S. Gibson's *Lochiel of the '45.*

Details of the works referred to above are included in the following bibliography, which includes other printed primary sources, and a selection of secondary works consulted. Most are widely available in good libraries. In addition, the National Library of Scotland has a considerable collection of manuscripts, printed ephemera and engravings of relevance to the '45, and Jacobitism generally. The Library's Antiquarian Books Division also has a number of richly-bound volumes from the private collections of Prince Charles and his brother Henry, Cardinal York.

BIBLIOGRAPHY

ADAM, R.J., 'The Northern Campaign of the 45: The Story of a Little War', *History Today,* vol VIII, no. 6 (June 1958)

ALLARDYCE, James, Colonel, *Historical Papers Relating to the Jacobite Period 1699-1750,* 2 vols, New Spalding Club (Aberdeen, 1895-6)

ATHOLL, John, 7th Duke of, *Chronicles of the Atholl and Tullibardine Families,* 5 vols (Edinburgh, 1908), vol 3

An authentick account of the conduct of the Young Chevalier: from his first arrival in Paris, after his defeat at Cullodden, to the conclusion of the peace at Aix-la-Chapelle (London, 1749)

BLACK, J., ed., *British Foreign Policy in the Age of Walpole* (Edinburgh, 1985)

BLACK J., *Culloden and the '45* (Stroud, 1990)

BLAIKIE, Walter B., *Itinerary of Prince Charles Edward Stuart,* Scottish History Society, 1st series, no. XXIII (Edinburgh, 1897)

BLAIKIE, Walter B., ed., *Origins of the Forty-Five,* Scottish History Society, 2nd series, no. II (Edinburgh, 1916) [Includes several important contemporary accounts]

BROWNE, J., *A History of the Highlands and of the Highland Clans,* 4 vols (London, 1848-9)

CARLYLE, Rev. Alexander, Minister of Inveresk, *Autobiography* (Edinburgh, 2nd edition, 1860)

CHALMERS, G., *A Collection of Treaties between Great Britain and Other Powers,* 2 vols (London, 1790)

CHAMBERS, Robert, *History of the Rebellion of 1745-6* (Edinburgh, 1827; 7th edition, Edinburgh, 1869)

CHAMBERS, Robert, ed., *Jacobite Memoirs of the Rebellion of 1745* (Edinburgh, 1834) [Includes Lord George Murray's 'Marches of the Highland Army']

CHERRY, A., *Princes, Poets and Patrons* (Edinburgh, 1987)

CORDARA, Giulio C., *Commentary on the Expedition to Scotland made by Charles Edward Stuart, Prince of Wales,* ed. by Sir Bruce Gordon Seton,

Miscellany of the Scottish History Society (vol IV), 3rd series, no. IX (Edinburgh, 1926)

COXE, William, *Memoirs of the Life and Administration of Sir Robert Walpole*, 3 vols (London, 1800)

COXE, William, *Memoirs of the Administration of Henry Pelham*, 2 vols (London, 1829)

CRUICKSHANKS, Eveline, ed., *Ideology and Conspiracy: Aspects of Jacobitism, 1689-1759* (Edinburgh, 1982)

DAICHES, David, *Charles Edward Stuart: The Life and Times of Bonnie Prince Charlie* (London, 1973)

DENNISTOUN, James, ed., *Cochrane correspondence regarding the affairs of Glasgow 1745-46*, Maitland Club (Edinburgh, 1836)

DENNISTOUN, James, ed., *Memoirs of Sir Robert Strange and Andrew Lumisden*, 2 vols (London, 1855)

DUKE, Winifred, *Lord George Murray and the '45* (Aberdeen, 1927)

DUKE, Winifred, *Prince Charles Edward and the 'Forty-Five* (London, 1938)

DUFF, H.R., ed., *Culloden Papers* (London, 1815)

ELCHO, David Wemyss, Lord, *A Short Account of the Affairs of Scotland in the Years 1744, 1745, 1746*, ed. by the Hon. Evan Charteris (Edinburgh, 1907)

ERICKSON, Carolly, *Bonnie Prince Charlie* (New York, 1989)

FORSTER, Margaret, *The Rash Adventurer: the Rise and Fall of Charles Edward Stuart* (London, 1973)

FRASER, Sir William, *The Chiefs of Colquhoun*, 2 vols (Edinburgh, 1869)

FRASER, Sir William, *The Earls of Cromartie*, 2 vols (Edinburgh, 1876)

FRASER, Sir William, *The Chiefs of Grant*, 3 vols (Edinburgh, 1883)

FRASER, Sir William, *The Sutherland Book*, 3 vols (Edinburgh, 1892)

A Full Collection of all the Proclamations and Orders Published by the Authority of Charles, Prince of Wales (Glasgow, 1745-46)

GIBSON, John S., *Ships of the '45: The Rescue of the Young Pretender* (London, 1967)

GIBSON, John S., *Lochiel of the '45* (Edinburgh, 1994)

HENDERSON, Andrew, *The History of the Rebellion, 1745 & 1746* (Edinburgh, 1748)

HEPBURNE-SCOTT, Hon. G.F.C., ed., *Marchmont Correspondence relating to the '45*, Miscellany of the Scottish History Society (Vol V), 3rd series, no. XXI (Edinburgh, 1933)

HOME, John, *The History of the Rebellion in Scotland in 1745* (London, 1802)

HOOK, Michael, ed., *Lord Provost George Drummond 1687-1766*, Scotland's Cultural Heritage (Edinburgh, 1987)

HUME, David, *A True Account of the Behaviour and Conduct of Archibald Stewart, Esq., Late Lord Provost of Edinburgh* (London, 1748)

JARVIS, Rupert C., *Collected Papers on the Jacobite Risings*, 2 vols (Manchester, 1971-72)

JOHNSTONE, James, Chevalier de, *Memoirs of the Rebellion in 1745 and 1746* (London, 1822)

LANG, Andrew, *Prince Charles Edward* (London, 1903)

LA TREMOILLE, Charles Louis, Duc de, *A Royalist Family, Irish and French (1689-1789) and Prince Charles Edward*, translated by A.G. Murray MacGregor (Edinburgh, 1904) [Includes Captain Darbé's *Journal* on board the *Du Teillay*]

LEASK, J.C., & McCANCE, H.M., *The Regimental Records of the Royal Scots* (Dublin, 1915)

LENMAN, Bruce, *The Jacobite Risings in Britain, 1689-1746* (London, 1980)

LENMAN, Bruce, & GIBSON, John S., *The Jacobite Threat: England, Scotland, Ireland, France: A Source Book* (Edinburgh, 1990)

LIVINGSTONE, Alastair, of Bachuil, AIKMAN, Christian W.H., & HART, Betty Stuart, eds., *Muster Roll of Prince Charles Edward Stuart's Army, 1745-46* (Aberdeen, 1984)

LOCKHART, George, of Carnwath, *The Lockhart Papers*, ed. by Anthony Aufrere, 2 vols (London, 1817)

MacDONALD, Revs. A. & A., *The Clan Donald*, 3 vols (Inverness, 1896-1904)

MacKENZIE, Alexander, *History of the Camerons; with Genealogies of the Principal Families of the Name* (Inverness, 1884)

MacKENZIE, [Sir Edward Montague] Compton, *Prince Charlie* (London, 1932)

MacLACHLAN, A.N.C., *William Augustus, Duke of Cumberland* (London, 1876)

MacLEAN, Fitzroy, *Bonnie Prince Charlie* (London, 1988)

MARISCHAL, George Keith, 10th Earl, *Two Fragments of Autobiography*, ed. by J.Y.T. Greig, Miscellany of the Scottish History Society (vol V), 3rd series, no. XXI (1933)

MARSHALL, Rosalind K., *Bonnie Prince Charlie* (Edinburgh, 1988)

MAXWELL, James, of Kirkconnell, *Narrative of Charles Prince of Wales's expediton to Scotland in the year 1745*, Maitland Club (Edinburgh, 1841)

McLYNN, F.J., *France and the Jacobite Rebellion of 1745* (Edinburgh, 1981)

McLYNN, F.J., *The Jacobite Army in England* (Edinburgh, 1983)

McLYNN, F.J., *The Jacobites* (London, 1985)

McLYNN, F.J., *Charles Edward Stuart, A Tragedy in Many Acts* (London, 1988)

MENARY, G., *The Life and Letters of Duncan Forbes of Culloden* (London, 1936)

MILLAR, A.H., ed., *A Selection of Scottish Forfeited Estates Papers 1715; 1745*, Scottish History Society, 1st series, no. LVII (Edinburgh, 1909)

MITCHELL, A.A., 'London and the Forty-Five', *History Today*, Vol XV, no. 10 (October 1965)

MORITZ, [Hermann], Count of Saxony [Marshal Saxe], *The Art of War, Reveries and Memoirs* (London, 1811)

MUNRO, N., *The History of the Royal Bank of Scotland 1727-1927* (Edinburgh, 1928)

MURRAY, David, *The York Buildings Company*, (Glasgow, 1883; reprinted, Edinburgh, 1973)

MURRAY, John, of Broughton, *Memorials of John Murray of Broughton, Sometime Secretary to Prince Charles Edward 1740-1747,* ed. by Robert Fitzroy Bell, Scottish History Society, 1st series, no. XXVII (Edinburgh, 1898)

PATON, Henry, ed., *The Lyon in Mourning,* 3 vols, Scottish History Society, 1st series, nos. XX-XXII (Edinburgh 1895-6; reprinted 1975)

PETRIE, Sir Charles, *The Jacobite Movement* (London, 3rd edition 1959)

PRATT-INSH, G., *The Scottish Jacobite Movement* (Edinburgh, 1952)

PREBBLE, John, *Culloden* (London, 1961)

The Report of the Proceedings and Opinion of the Board of General Officers, on their examination into the conduct, behaviour and proceedings of Lieutenant-General Sir John Cope (London, 1749)

ROGERS N., 'Popular Disaffection in London during the '45', *London Journal,* vol I, no. 1 (May 1975)

ROSEBERY, Lord & MacLEOD, Rev. Walter, eds., *List of Persons concerned in the Rebellion,* Scottish History Society, 1st series, no. VIII (Edinburgh, 1890)

SCOTT, Sir Walter, *Waverley, Or, 'Tis Sixty Years Since,* 3 vols (Edinburgh, 1814)

SCOTT, Sir Walter, *The Tales of a Grandfather,* 3 vols (Edinburgh, 1827-30)

SETON, Sir Bruce Gordon, & ARNOT, Jean Gordon, eds., *The Prisoners of the '45,* 3 vols, Scottish History Society, 3rd series, nos. XIII-XV (Edinburgh, 1928-9)

SIMPSON, Llewellyn Eardley, *Derby and the Forty-Five* (London, 1933)

SMITH, Annette M., *Jacobite Estates of the Forty-Five* (Edinburgh, 1982)

SPECK, W.A., *The Butcher: the Duke of Cumberland and the Suppression of the Forty-Five* (Oxford, 1981)

STEUART, Archibald F., ed., *The Woodhouselee manuscript. A narrative of events in Edinburgh and district during the Jacobite occupation, September to November 1745* (London, 1907)

TAYLER, Alistair & Henrietta, *1745 and after* (London, 1938) [John William OSullivan's 'Narrative']

TAYLER, Alistair & Henrietta, *The Stuart Papers at Windsor* (London, 1939)

TAYLER, Henrietta, *Jacobite Epilogue* (London, 1941)

TAYLER, Henrietta, *Bonnie Prince Charlie* (London, 1945)[A biography for children]

TAYLER, Henrietta, *A Jacobite Miscellany,* Roxburghe Club (London, 1948) [Includes Prince Charles's own account of the '45]

TAYLER, Henrietta, *Two Accounts of the Escape of Prince Charles Edward* (Oxford, 1951)

TERRY, Charles S., ed., *Albemarle Papers,* 2 vols, New Spalding Club, (Aberdeen, 1902)

TOMASSON, Katherine, *The Jacobite General* (Edinburgh, 1958)

TOMASSON, Katherine, & BUIST, Francis, *Battles of the '45* (London, 1962)

WARRAND, Duncan, ed., *More Culloden Papers,* 5 vols (Inverness, 1923-30)

The Whole Proceedings in the House of Peers, upon the impeachment exhibited... against Simon, Lord Lovat for High Treason — March 1746-7 (London, 1747)

YORKE, P. C., *The Life and Correspondence of Philip Yorke, Earl of Hardwicke, Lord High Chancellor of Great Britain*, 3 vols (Cambridge, 1913)

The Young Chevalier, or a Genuine Narrative of all that befell that Unfortunate Adventurer (London, 1750)

YOUNGSON, A. J., *After the Forty-Five: The Economic Impact on the Scottish Highlands* (Edinburgh, 1973)

YOUNGSON, A. J., *The Prince and the Pretender* (London, 1985)

INDEX

[Page numbers within brackets denote illustrations]